The Positive Mentality
Time management, sleep & positive routines

Summary

Time management skills include a wide range of abilities that will assist you in effectively managing your time. Some of the most significant time management skills are reprioritization, organization, delegation and communication. Developing these skills can help you achieve your objectives and become an effective time manager. Time may be monitored in a variety of ways, from manually inputting the start and finish times to employing complex time tracking and project management software. When tracking time, it is critical to record not just the number of hours worked but also the activities accomplished, the customers for whom you worked, and the projects completed.

One handy method is to maintain an Activity Log, which we'll look at in this course. When you fully comprehend how you spend your time at work, you may reduce or eliminate low-value tasks. This implies you can perform more high-value work while still leaving the workplace at a reasonable hour. Activity Logs should not be confused with timesheets; they are used for reporting on your time use and recording the time you spend on a task or work.

They are also beneficial for identifying non-core activities that do not help you reach critical goals. For example, you may spend significantly more time than you realize perusing the web or grabbing coffee each afternoon. You may also notice that you are more energized in certain parts of the day and less energetic in others. Efficient time management is one of the most crucial abilities for busy entrepreneurs to have to keep their companies running smoothly.

As an entrepreneur, you may have multiple meetings to attend as well as other things to do throughout the day. Set a hard stop time when such unanticipated occurrences occur. Focus on one job at a time is the most effective strategy to do more tasks. Having your complete concentration on one activity increases efficiency, which increases production. Business productivity is often defined as revenue divided by hours worked.

Productivity assesses how successful firms create money from inputs such as labour and materials. An aggregate productivity level is unlikely to give practical insights to corporate executives, but it may assist them to assess how they compare to competitors or other top organizations. The six degrees of productivity that we think individuals experience at work are listed below. The value may be difficult to establish, but you may begin by considering the results. Not every job on your to-do list is equal in terms of the value it provides to you or others.

You can accomplish one unit of labour and get fifty units of output while doing game-changing work. Highly productive individuals understand where their energy is best spent and can concentrate their attention accordingly. They minimize time spent on "busy work" or low-value things such as endlessly scanning the web. Highly productive individuals have processes in place to locate what they need when they want it. Mobile applications specialized in your sector may assist you in staying on top of a variety of issues.

If you're not cautious, applications, email, and other technology may become distractions rather than productivity helps. Productive individuals invest in the necessary tools to help their companies grow. If businesses still use paper forms for things like invoicing, purchase orders, and staff scheduling, you may save time and money by switching to mobile forms and a secure cloud-based storage solution. The list should be as closely connected with our philosophy, values, and personality as possible. Once you've decided on a goal, it's much simpler to pursue it since you have that internal driving component.

Table of Content

Chapter 1: Preparation for effective time management
Chapter 1.1: Time Management Skills
Chapter 1.2: Effectively Manage Time
Chapter 1.3: Change Your Laziness
Chapter 1.4: Necessity of Routines
Chapter 1.5: Set Your Routine
Chapter 1.6: Time Management and Sleep

Chapter 2: Guide to time management strategies
Chapter 2.1: Track Your Time
Chapter 2.2: Track Your Activity
Chapter 2.3: Time Management Strategies
Chapter 2.4: How to Organize and Manage Your Time
Chapter 2.5: Time Management for Beginners
Chapter 2.6: How to Ensure Productivity Through Time Management

Chapter 3: Time Management for Different Personnel
Chapter 3.1: Time Management for Entrepreneurs
Chapter 3.2: Time Management for Single Moms
Chapter 3.3: Time Management for Writers
Chapter 3.4: Time Management for High School Students

Chapter 4: Track yourself to understand yourself better
Chapter 4.1: Control Your Day
Chapter 4.2: Control Your Life
Chapter 4.3: Positive Routines
Chapter 4.4: Track Your Daily Habits
Chapter 4.5: Track Your Goals

Chapter 5: Work on Personal Development
Chapter 5.1: Positive Mentality
Chapter 5.2: Control Your Mindset
Chapter 5.3: Fix Your Obsessions
Chapter 5.4: Avoid Distractions
Chapter 5.5: Set Daily Goals

Chapter 6: All about Productivity
Chapter 6.1: Productivity and Productivity Levels
Chapter 6.2: Professional Productivity
Chapter 6.3: Long-Term Productivity
Chapter 6.4: Productivity in Economics
Chapter 6.5: Product Management
Chapter 6.6: Workplace Productivity

Chapter 7: maximize your work productivity
Chapter 7.1: Learn Smart Strategies
Chapter 7.2: Minimum Input Maximum Output
Chapter 7.3: How to Improve Work Efficiency to Increase Productivity
Chapter 7.4: Business Management

Chapter 8: Masterpiece Being Productive & Living Principle
Chapter 8.1: How to Find True Happiness and Inner Peace
Chapter 8.2: How to Work Less and Get More Done
Chapter 8.3: Improve Your Work Environment and Optimize Productivity
Chapter 8.4: The Secret to Handle Difficult and Toxic People
Chapter 8.5: How to Build and Sustain a Healthy and Purposeful Relationship

CHAPTER 1: PREPARATION FOR EFFECTIVE TIME MANAGEMENT

Chapter 1.1: Time Management Skills

Time management skills include a wide range of abilities that will assist you in effectively managing your time. Among the most significant time management skills are:

Organization

Staying organized may help you keep track of what you need to do and when you need to do it. Being well-organized may include keeping an up-to-date schedule, being able to readily access certain papers, keeping a clean atmosphere, and taking precise, careful notes.

Prioritization

Being an effective time manager requires you to prioritize each of your obligations. There are several methods for prioritizing what has to be done. You may choose to accomplish quick, easy tasks first, followed by longer, more difficult tasks. Alternatively, you might prioritise your jobs by priority, beginning with the most time-sensitive, or a mix of the two.

Goal-setting

Setting objectives is the first step toward being an effective time manager. Objective-setting enables you to grasp your final goal and what you need to prioritize to achieve it. Setting both short-term and long-term objectives may contribute to job success.

Communication

Developing great communication skills may help you communicate your objectives and goals to others with whom you work. It also enables you to delegate, allowing you to concentrate on the most critical, relevant activities that match your objectives.

Planning

Planning is an essential component of time management. Being efficient in arranging your day, meetings, and how you will complete tasks can help you stay on track.

Delegation

Being competent in time management entails just performing tasks that will assist you and your organization achieve your objectives. While managers are more likely to exercise this skill, if you are in charge of a project, you may also practice delegating work. While it might be tough to say "no" when someone asks you to do something at work, it is important to practice setting boundaries to manage your time effectively and achieve your objectives.

Stress management

You should be mindful of your mental health while practising effective time management. Healthily handling stress might help you remain motivated and perform well throughout your day. You may do this by taking tiny breaks throughout the day or rewarding yourself in modest ways as you complete chores.

Taking the time to develop each of these abilities can help you manage your daily work, whether you are working, looking for employment, or attempting to learn a new talent.

Chapter 1.2: Effectively Manage Time

Let's have a look at some best practices for better time management right now.

#1 Create a system that you like using and looking at for effective time management.

The most efficient strategy to manage time is to design systems that work for you and make you happy every time you look at them. If you prefer 'old-fashioned' pen and paper, make a to-do list on it. It's OK if you like apps or want everything on your calendar. The crucial thing is that you enjoy your system so that you interact with it rather than avoid it. If you don't like the system you're using, you'll be reluctant to open it and use it, which will work against your productivity.

#2 Time Management Best Practice: Be Realistic

It's one thing to desire to do everything; it's quite another to be realistic about what you can accomplish and the time limit in which you can accomplish it. Effective time management entails controlling expectations realistically. One method is to look at the work at hand and estimate how many hours it will take to complete. Then divide the hours by days, performing a little work each day until the assignment is finished.

For example, if you have a major job that you believe will need ten hours to complete, look at your schedule and determine when you can devote those hours. Can you commit to two hours of work each morning for the next five days? Can you commit to one hour each day for ten days or three hours per week for three weeks? Be practical, and then follow through on your decision.

#3 How to Manage Time: Work When You Work Best

It is not enough to have a to-do list; you must also create time in your day to concentrate on that list, at times that are appropriate for the activity at hand.

For example, if you have a project that demands a lot of attention and you work best in the morning, schedule time to work on it in the morning. Even if it's just for three hours, work on things while you're at your best.

Don't simply put it on your to-do list and believe you'll get to it eventually.

#4 Time Management Tip: Create a 'Filler List

There are usually intervals throughout the day from the more serious work, and one of the easiest methods to enhance productivity is to fill such intervals with a few smaller tasks on the to-do list. This is referred to as the 'filler list' by some. These are tasks that must be completed but do not need hours or a calm environment. Perhaps it's sending a few text messages, responding to emails, or making phone calls you've been putting off.

Consider all of the 15–20-minute blocks of time you have in a day. If you sum it all up, you have at least 1-2 hours to go through a lot of stuff.

#5 Break It Down: How to Manage Time Effectively

Part of the reason we don't have good time management is that we frequently don't want to perform work that is too difficult, so we wait for it to go away, or we put it off, or we put it on the list as a full project, but never get to it. This leads to procrastination, and according to experts, procrastination is more emotional than logistical.

Tips from the Experts on How to Manage Time More Effectively

According to time management experts such as Robby Slaughter, workflow and productivity expert, and speaker on topics related to personal productivity and corporate efficiency, the problem most of us face when attempting to increase productivity is that we focus too much on time and tasks and not enough on relationships and impact. Time management isn't only about practicalities; it's also about ensuring our mental well-being, which is why Robby suggests we build something nice into our weekly routine so we have something to look forward to.

Chapter 1.3: Change Your Laziness

Have you ever had so many things to accomplish that you didn't want to get up from the couch? Do you wish to go above your current abilities to fight idleness and go to work? Do you want to quit sighing from exhaustion? Forget about the terror and dread of the numerous duties stacking up right in front of you. Every issue has a solution.

If you fall into this category and are ready to finally free yourself of lethargy, it's time to make a change! Don't put anything off until "Sunday." Go straight to the objective you set for yourself. Here are some helpful hints for replacing negative habits with healthy ones and eventually getting rid of idleness.

Is laziness procrastination?

Procrastination is not the same as laziness (desire to work less). Procrastination aids in the division of labour into tiny and simple jobs. Procrastination, according to experts, has a good influence on the employee's talents and inventiveness. All of history's geniuses - inventors and many mathematicians - want to make their job simpler, to avoid spending time on unnecessary and mundane tasks. However, laziness is defined as a reluctance to accomplish anything.

How to fight against laziness?

Try to understand why you are lazy

You won't be able to address the issue if you don't know what's causing it. A person might become indolent for a variety of reasons. It might be a challenging chore, so difficult to do that you just do not want to work. Your motivation will be utterly destroyed by a sense of impotence and a lack of energy. Here are a few such examples:

Tiresome and boring task

People have become used to dealing with such challenges throughout their lives. From arduous physics and chemistry activities to mundane daily chores to huge corporate operations. People are obliged to do things they do not want to do throughout their life.

But think at it this way: you can't live in shambles. You can't eat nutritious meals if you don't cook every day. You won't be able to pass an essential test or acquire the job of your dreams if you don't study. Everything has a cost, and routine is the cost of success.

Make a strategy to perform all normal duties. Plan your day such that the exciting things become uninteresting and vice versa. Consider the repercussions as well: what will happen if you do nothing?

Fear activates laziness

Sometimes you can't finish a job right immediately. You are concerned that you will not be able to complete the task in time. Fear puts strain on you. Your intuition and instincts predict the problem that is causing your productivity to suffer. You want to abandon your whole company and go someplace far away.

Consider that and try to figure out why you are so afraid. You'll feel better if you do this. The most important thing is to believe in yourself, and you will be successful in everything.

Fatigue

Do you want to go to work but are too exhausted to move even your muscles? You might have major health issues, consume bad foods, or just exercise a little. Make an effort to transform your today!

Get up on time, prepare a nutritious breakfast, and enjoy a cup of green tea. Warm up by going for a morning stroll or doing a series of exercises. You might perhaps go for a bike ride or to the gym.

Believe me, the following day you will feel much better and be ready for new work wins since you cannot feel weary when you are full of vitality.

Set clear goals

You have no idea what to do or where to go if you don't have any objectives. Goals are your road map, so identify what you want to accomplish in every aspect of your life. Do not let a single day go by in vain.

Here's an example: Take a piece of paper and write down who you want to be or what you want to accomplish in the next 5 or 10 years.

Routine – useful!

Plan your perfect day now that you've set your objectives. Make a list of all the key actions to be completed on that day, and schedule a time to finish them. All of these everyday duties will no longer feel onerous after you've gotten adjusted to your new schedule.

Divide a large task into several smaller ones

Sometimes it is even unclear which side of the large issue should be handled. So break it down into smaller jobs. Try not to see it as something large and hefty. Pay attention to the details.

You can apply this principle to everything!

Do you purchase new furnishings and clothing? The mere notion of a protracted hunt for acceptable items that you can't live without might put you under stress. Only solve one issue every day. Do you need footwear? Purchase them right now! Do you need a new jacket? Purchase it now! Spend just 15 minutes every day on such things to avoid becoming bored with them.

Get away from lazy people

Keep in mind that your interlocutors have an impact on your thoughts and lifestyle. If the individuals you spend most of your time with are lazy, you will feel lethargic as well. Conversely, if you interact with busy and successful individuals, their energy will be transmitted to you. You'll be motivated, and you'll want to thrive.

Use laziness as a reward

Overcoming laziness is not tough, particularly if you treat yourself sometimes. After you have accomplished all of your daily responsibilities, reward yourself. Watch TV and use social media. All of these activities keep you from working successfully, yet they are enjoyable and beneficial outside of the workplace.

Look for inspiration and motivation

Read books by successful entrepreneurs, listen to positive individuals, and do everything that will motivate you and improve your life.

It is up to you to decide where your life will go. Only you have control over who and what you become. Fight against laziness. Become prosperous.

Chapter 1.4: Necessity of Routines

You get up an hour early to get ready for work. You wash quickly and grab an energy bar and a cup of coffee before rushing out the door. Work, on the other hand, leaves you feeling disoriented and overburdened. You're exhausted towards the end of the week and know you won't meet your objectives for the week.

How can you pull yourself out of this rut? Routines, in a nutshell.

Morning and evening routines help you succeed. They assist you in doing more, thinking clearly, and doing meaningful work. They save you from fumbling through your day and ensure that you do the most critical tasks.

It just takes a little discipline, as well as habits that will set you up for success. Here's the what and why of routines, as well as 12 morning and evening routines you may use to make your days more flawless.

The Science of Habits and Creating Routines

To begin, let us define routine: A routine is a series of activities that you perform regularly.

Brushing your teeth and getting ready for bed is a habit. Every morning at 6:00 a.m., I get up and exercise. Buying a bagel and reading the news before heading to work is a daily ritual. It's even a habit to munch chips while watching Netflix. They are all acts that occur repeatedly, creating a rhythm in your everyday life.

That doesn't make them all excellent routines; they're just routines since they're done regularly. Every routine, whether helpful or not, is powerful.

Routines Create High Achievers

"We are what we repeatedly do. Excellence, then, is not an act, but a habit." ---- **Aristotle**

Mason Currey writes on the habits, routines, and rituals of hundreds of artists, including Frederic Chopin, Benjamin Franklin, Karl Marx, and Ernest Hemingway, in his book Daily Rituals: How Artists Work. Even though their routines differed greatly, each person had actions they took to put themselves in the best possible mental condition.

Currey came to the following conclusion after examining the great artists:

In the proper hands, [a routine] may be a finely tuned mechanism for maximizing a variety of limited resources, including time (the most restricted resource of them), willpower, self-discipline, and optimism. A consistent schedule creates a well-worn groove for one's mental energy and aids in avoiding the tyranny of emotions.

Tim Ferris, productivity guru, and experimenter extraordinaire have five-morning routines that help him get into a productive mindset: making his bed, meditating, exercising, sipping tea, and writing. Tony Robbins, a performance coach, prepares for each day with a daily ritual that involves a cold shower, breathing exercises, and meditation.

High achievers usually develop routines that work for them and keep to them—usually, it's something they attribute to their success.

Routines vs. Habits vs. Rituals: Do you know the distinction between habits, routines, and rituals? Habits are something we do habitually, such as checking email first thing in the morning or placing our keys in a set location when we return home. Routines are often a set of behaviour or action that you do regularly to bring order to your day—for example, reading your email, then composing your day's to-do list, and then checking your team's project management application to start the day. Rituals are similar to routines. The major distinction is the mentality behind the actions: Taking a stroll at lunchtime every day may be called a habit if you consider it something you must do for your productivity. It might also be a ritual if you consider it a method to get away from every day and appreciate nature. While we're on the subject of habits and routines, most routines may be transformed into rituals with a shift of attitude.

Routines Put Our Brains on Autopilot

But what makes great achievers' habits so effective? As it turns out, we are creatures of habit, and we can utilize that to our advantage. Charles Duhigg describes how habits push our brains into an automatic state where little or no effort is necessary in his book The Power of Habit: Why We Do What We Do in Life and Business.

It operates as follows:

- **Step 1:** Something occurs that acts as a stimulus to your brain, causing it to go into "automatic" mode. A basic example would be waking awake. When I wake up, my brain tells me it's time to start the coffee machine. This behaviour has been imprinted in my mind over time.

- **Step 2:** Carry out the routine. This is where I start the coffee machine, wait for it to boil, pour it into my favourite cup, sit in a chair by the kitchen window, and enjoy the coffee.

- **Step #3:** Reap the benefits of regularity. The exquisite taste and high-octane caffeine reinforce the pattern, so I repeat it the following morning.

Making coffee is simply one tiny ritual, but the daily repetition keeps me going. Imagine if other, more powerful actions that might enable you to do great things were as simple as preparing coffee.

This is the strength of routines. Small, repetitive acts may have a huge impact. Develop morning and evening routines to prepare yourself for maximum productivity each day.

Chapter 1.5: Set Your Routine

Rise Early

There are outliers, such as Winston Churchill, who preferred to stay in bed until 11:00 a.m., but many top achievers get up early to prepare for the day. They may carry out their rituals when the rest of the world is sleeping.

Consider the following examples:

- Square CEO Jack Dorsey gets up at 5:30 a.m. to go for a 6 jog.
- Richard Branson, the founder of Virgin Group, gets up at 5:45 a.m. to exercise and have a nutritious breakfast.
- GM CEO Dan Akerson gets up between 4:30 and 5:00 a.m. to speak with GE Asia.
- Tim Cook, CEO of Apple, wakes up at 4:30 a.m. to write emails and go to the gym by 5:00 a.m.

Even if they aren't naturally morning larks (the polar opposite of night owls), they've taught themselves to get up early for the numerous advantages that come with it. Increased productivity with fewer interruptions in the early morning, higher creativity since you can work while your mind is fresh, and reduced stress if you utilize that additional time for meditation or silent contemplation is some of the benefits. It may also make you happier: In one study, researchers discovered that morning people had greater levels of optimism and well-being.

Tip: Even if you're a night owl, you may teach yourself to be a morning person by getting up 20 minutes earlier every day and getting some sunshine as soon as you wake up.

Make Your Bed

Making your bed every day is one habit you should develop to enhance your life. At least, that's what Navy Seal Admiral William H. McCraven says:

You will have completed the first chore of the day if you make your bed every morning. It will offer you a little sensation of accomplishment and will motivate you to do another chore, then another, and another. And by the end of the day, that one-done work will have multiplied into numerous accomplished tasks.

Making your bed will also highlight the importance of the simple things in life. You'll never be able to accomplish the big things correctly if you can't do the small things right. And if you have a bad day, you'll return home to a bed that is made - that you made. And a made bed offers you hope for a better day tomorrow.

It's all about the small things.

Recite Affirmations

Affirmations are positive affirmations that you may use to change your thoughts about yourself and your day ahead. They are a method of envisioning and conquering negative self-talk by imagining the wonderful things that will happen to you that day.

In his book *The Miracle Morning: The Not-So-Obvious Secret Guaranteed to Transform Your Life (Before 8 AM)*, Hal Elrod says:

When you consciously plan and write down your affirmations to be in sync with what you want to achieve and whom you need to be to achieve it, then commit to repeating them regularly (preferably out loud), they have an instant imprint on your subconscious mind. Your affirmations work to change the way you think and feel, allowing you to overcome limiting beliefs and habits and replace them with ones that will help you achieve.

You might use the following basic affirmations:

- I will do great things today
- I will make $XXX this year
- I am a highly respected [insert occupation]
- I am achieving [big goal]

The goal is to confirm and picture what you wish to happen. As you concentrate on these things, you will begin to think that you can and will attain them, allowing you to take action.

Get some exercise

Few things are more transforming than exercise. Morning exercise boosts blood flow, produces endorphins, and strengthens the body. It gets you ready for the day ahead, boosts your energy levels, and helps you stay healthy. Numerous research has indicated that exercise is important in combating melancholy and anxiety, and one Finnish study even claimed that exercise is associated with increasing income.

Eat a proper breakfast

The fuel you ingest first thing in the morning has a huge impact on your whole performance, thus it should be the best fuel available.

Dieticians advise avoiding high-sugar, high-fat meals in favour of healthier options, such as:

- Oatmeal
- Low-fat breakfast sandwich
- Smoothie
- Fruit and yoghurt parfait

Consider excellent carbohydrates and fibre, as well as some protein. These items will provide you with energy and fulfil your food desires while setting the tone for positive selections throughout the day.

Take a cold shower

This may sound a bit excessive, but many people swear by taking cold showers first thing in the morning. It's comparable to sportsmen taking ice baths, although not quite as cold.

Why take a cold shower? Because it may improve blood flow, burn fat, and release dopamine into the body. It, like exercise, jumpstarts your body.

This is why Tony Robbins immerses himself in 57-degree water every morning. He is certain that it is necessary for optimal productivity.

Evening Routines to Set the Tone for the Following Day

The end of each day is just as vital as the beginning. By establishing nighttime rituals, you prepare yourself for the following morning, recharge with a night of peaceful sleep, and reduce the reluctance to get things done.

Prepare goals for the next day

It enables you to determine your most critical duties ahead of time before the stresses of the day come. Ideally, you should spend the first several hours of each day on your most difficult assignment. This concept has been variously referred to as "eating the frog" and "slaying the dragon."

Reflect on the day's achievements

After a long day, it's easy to lose sight of your accomplishments. Taking a few minutes at the end of the day to reflect on and celebrate your victories puts things into perspective and provides you with motivation for the next day. It assists you in overcoming the despondency that is sometimes associated with defeats.

Clear your head

It's easy to carry your work to bed, making it harder to sleep while you think about work-related issues. Clearing your thoughts before going to bed enables you to set aside the stresses of the day and prepare your mind to sleep. There are many methods to do this, including:

- Meditation
- Light reading
- Playing Tetris (for productivity!)
- Watching a peaceful television show (*The Walking Dead* probably isn't your best bet)
- Doing a "brain dump" of all the thoughts in your head in a journal before you go to bed

Your objective is to divert your attention away from work-related activities.

Prepare for the next morning

Take the time to arrange things in the morning to reduce the amount of thinking you have to do. Prepare the food you'll eat, prepare the coffeemaker, and arrange any work-related items you'll need to bring. If you're heading to the gym, have your exercise clothes and water ready.

The less time and mental energy you devote to trivial matters, the more time and mental energy you will have for the things that matter.

Tidy up

A filthy house isn't the most inspirational way to start the day. You'll rapidly discover your house in chaos if you don't tidy up and put things away regularly.

Fortunately, spending only 10 to 20 minutes a night tidying up will help minimise morning tension and help you avoid long cleaning marathons on weekends. If you only do one thing, make it cleaning and shining your sink. This one chore, like making your bed in the morning, will offer you a feeling of success. FlyLady, a housekeeping expert, says:

This is your very first housekeeping task. Many of you are perplexed as to why I want you to clear your sink of filthy dishes and clean and shine it when you have so much more to accomplish. It's so easy; I want you to feel proud of yourself! [...] When you wake up the following morning, your sink will welcome you with a grin on your wonderful face. I can't offer you a huge hug, but I know how satisfying it is to see yourself in your kitchen sink.

Go shine your sink!

Practice proper sleep hygiene

Few individuals exercise adequate sleep hygiene, and as a consequence, their sleep suffers. As a general rule, you should:

- Maintain the same sleep and waking pattern.
- Reduce blue light from displays (this can be done using F.lux on your computer and "Night Mode" on your mobile device).
- Set your room temperature between 60- and 65 degrees Fahrenheit (15 and 18 degrees Celsius).
- Make sure your room is as dark as possible.

It's tempting to dismiss the value of sleep, yet it's necessary for peak performance. Sleep is so important that Arianna Huffington dedicated an entire Ted Talk to it.

To develop your morning and evening routines, make a checklist that you can go through every day until it becomes second nature to you, or put up a plan like Ben Franklin. As an example:

- *6 am: wake, make the bed, get the coffee started*
- *6:15: read the news while drinking coffee*
- *6:30: exercise*
- *7: eat breakfast*

- *7:15: shower*
- *8-5: work*
- *6: dinner*
- *7:30: tidy up*
- *8: family time, television, or other forms of leisure and amusement*
- *9:30: journaling or meditation*
- *10: bedtime*

Chapter 1.6: Time Management and Sleep

People often forego sleep to complete other responsibilities, such as preparing for an exam or finishing a professional assignment. While cutting down on sleep may help you reach your objectives, those missed hours add up and may have an impact on your overall productivity. Sleep deprivation impairs concentration and makes it difficult to operate throughout the day. You may be able to enhance your sleep by better organising your time.

According to Dr Alicia Roth, a behavioural sleep expert, "Insufficient Sleep Syndrome develops when a person actively limits their time in bed and sleep." This might be due to a multitude of factors, such as working late into the night, students studying or working numerous jobs. People suffering from Insufficient Sleep Syndrome do not prioritise sleep."

Effects of Stress

Over 70 million Americans suffer from sleep deprivation, which has no one cause. People may have difficulty sleeping due to bad sleeping habits or as a side effect of the medicine. Sleep is greatly influenced by stress.

Adults with high-stress levels struggle with sleep, according to the American Psychological Association, getting fewer than seven hours of sleep and often waking up throughout the night. This is because it is more difficult for the body to wind down for sleep when you are agitated before bed.

When we are distressed, our bodies create more cortisol. Cortisol is a stress hormone that regulates the fight-or-flight response. When the body detects danger, the heart rate and blood pressure rise and certain muscles stiffen.

We may not feel this way every time we are anxious, but we are still tense, and it may take some time for us to relax. As a consequence, falling asleep takes longer, particularly when our attention is focused on what has to be done.

Sleep and Time

When we don't manage our time well, we often forgo sleep to do last-minute assignments. As a consequence, we have difficulty falling asleep since our bodies have greater cortisol levels and less melatonin.

Melatonin is a hormone that regulates the circadian rhythm, often known as the sleep-wake cycle. The production of melatonin is greatest at night and lowest during the day. Melatonin slows our bodies down and prepares them for sleep, but melatonin fails to help us sleep when cortisol levels are high.

We're also more prone to stress when we don't get enough sleep. This is why it is important to obtain adequate sleep to minimize stress and increase attention. Instead of foregoing sleep, relaxation is essential for increased productivity.

Avoid sacrificing your sleep. Following these easy actions may assist you in getting the rest you need to perform at your best.

- **Find out how much sleep you need**

Based on your age, our sleep calculator can determine how much sleep you need. It also gives you the best and worst times to go to bed depending on your waking time.

- **Keep a sleep schedule**

A night of consistent sleep and waking time creates a natural pattern, making it simpler to fall asleep and wake up in the morning. On weekends, stick to this sleep regimen. It may seem appealing to sleep in a few additional hours, but doing so may have a detrimental impact.

- **Avoid certain foods**

Foods heavy in sugar, fat, and spice may be difficult to digest soon before night. When you crawl into bed, your body may be more concerned with digesting than with preparation for sleep.

Chapter 2: Guide to Time Management Strategies

Chapter 2.1: Track Your Time

You must measure and record the number of hours worked to monitor time. This information is used to assess a company's efficiency and productivity.

Time may be monitored in a variety of ways, from manually inputting the start and finish times to employing complex time tracking and project management software. When tracking time, it is critical to record not just the number of hours worked but also the activities accomplished, the customers for whom you worked, and the projects completed.

How to Keep Track of Time Worked?

Paper Timesheets

The paper technique is the most basic approach to keeping track of time. Simply jot down your tasks, the business purpose, and how much time you spend executing them. Time may be tracked in 15-minute or 30-minute increments. This is ideal for usage everywhere, even if there is no internet connection.

The main issue with timesheets is that they are prone to mistakes since you might forget to input specific activities and other data, particularly when switching between projects. It might be tough to keep tangible records if you use them to monitor time for workers.

Spreadsheets

Excel spreadsheets may also be used to monitor time. This saves time and effort from having to create a real timesheet.

The advantage of utilizing digital spreadsheets is that once you've created a template, you can reuse it for different projects. Spreadsheets, unlike paper timesheets, may be efficiently backed up and stored. They also enable you to produce data reports.

While the spreadsheet is a superior way to measure time, it does not reflect the time spent on the work. It might become tiresome and time-consuming to manually input your time each time.

Time Tracking Software

Time monitoring tools and project management software enable you to keep track of how much time you spend on each work.

Small enterprises and freelancers who charge by the hour are the most likely users of the program. When you begin writing, start a clock and stop it when you finish. Some applications monitor time automatically in the background.

Before you decide to utilize mobile or desktop time monitoring tools, be sure they are appropriate for your company's goals and budget. Choose a system that is straightforward to set up, has an easy-to-use interface, allows for seamless connections, and can create comprehensive reports. You should be able to manage timesheets for your staff and allocate time to tasks.

What Is the Best Time Tracking App?

If you've opted to download a time-tracking system, you have a wealth of alternatives to pick from.

Asana

Asana, a popular project management application, assists you and your team in staying focused on projects, daily tasks, and objectives.

Boomr

Boomr allows you to conveniently monitor work hours from any device. Not only will you get real-time data, but you will also be able to automate timesheets, employee payroll reports, and overtime notifications.

Teamwork Projects

Teamwork Projects is a cloud-based project management system, that allows you to view precisely how much time your team is spending on projects. It includes several amazing productivity features including multiple timers, imminent task import, auto pause, and configurable time tracking.

Basecamp

Basecamp is a project management platform that helps you organise your projects, clients, and communication.

Trello

Trello's boards, lists, and cards allow you to organise and prioritise your work in an enjoyable, flexible, and rewarding manner.

Daycast

Daycast enables you to arrange your days so that you may focus on high-value initiatives and properly measure your time while maintaining the flexibility to pivot or reroute as required.

Businesses that have switched to a time-tracking system have seen a variety of advantages, ranging from a better knowledge of how your workdays are spent to more accurate billing rates, better project processes, and more transparency.

Chapter 2.2: Track Your Activity

How much time do you waste at work on activities that don't help you succeed? "Not much," you could remark at first. However, if you've never utilised Activity Logs before, you may be astonished at how much additional time you can find.

When you fully comprehend how you spend your time at work, you may reduce or eliminate low-value tasks. This implies you can perform more high-value work while still leaving the workplace at a reasonable hour.

So, how can you make sense of this? One handy method is to maintain an Activity Log, which is what we'll look at in this course.

About Activity Logs

An Activity Log (sometimes spelt Activity Diary or Job Activity Log) is a written record of how you spend your time.

By maintaining an Activity Log for a few days, you may get a good idea of what you do throughout the day and how you spend your time. You'll discover that memory is a terrible guide, and maintaining the Log is an eye-opening experience!

Your Activity Log will also assist you in determining whether or not you are doing your most critical tasks at the appropriate time of day. For example, if you're more active and creative in the morning, you should accomplish your most essential job then. In the afternoon, you may devote your attention to lower-intensity chores such as replying to emails or answering phone calls.

Activity logs are also beneficial for identifying non-core activities that do not help you reach critical goals. For example, you may spend significantly more time than you realize perusing the web or grabbing coffee each afternoon. When you realize how much time you're spending on such things, you may adjust your working habits to remove them.

Tip: Activity Logs should not be confused with timesheets; they are used for reporting on your time use and recording the time you spend on a task or work.

How to Keep an Activity Log

Download this **template** or start a new spreadsheet and add the following column headings to maintain an Activity Log:

- Date/Time.
- Activity description.
- How I feel.
- Duration.
- Value (high, medium, low, none).

Then, without modifying your behaviour any more than necessary, write down everything you do at work as you do it.

Every time you switch tasks, whether it's responding to an email, working on a report, making coffee, or talking with coworkers, write down what you're doing, when you switched, and how you felt (alert, flat, tired, energetic, and so on).

Then, at a later time, go back through your Activity Log and record the length of each activity as well as whether it was a high, medium, low, or no-value task. (Assess how far it contributed to accomplishing your employment objectives.)

Learning From Your Activity Log

Analyze your Activity Log after logging your time for a few days. You may be surprised to learn how much time you spend on low-value tasks!

You may also notice that you are more energized in certain parts of the day and less energetic in others. A lot of this might rely on how you are, the rest breaks you take, when and what you eat, and the task that you're performing.

After reviewing your Activity Log, you should be able to increase your productivity by implementing one of the following steps to different activities:

1. Jobs that aren't part of your function or that don't assist you accomplish your goals should be eliminated or delegated. Tasks that someone else in the business should be performing (perhaps at a lower pay rate) or personal hobbies such as sending non-work e-mails or browsing the Internet may fall into this category.

2. Schedule your most difficult duties during the times of day when you have the greatest energy. As a result, your work will be of higher quality and will take less time to complete.

3. Reduce the number of times you transition between task kinds. Could you, for example, read and respond to e-mails just a few times a day, or handle all of your bills at the same time each week?

4. Reduce your time spent on genuine personal tasks like preparing beverages. (Take turns doing this in your team - it saves time and builds team spirit!)

Chapter 2.3: Time Management Strategies

What exactly is time management? Is it a boss directing you on how to spend your time? Or is it just keeping oneself as busy as possible to maintain optimal production levels?

The fact is that managing time intelligently enough to get everything done as required without placing too much strain on oneself is a delicate balance.

You'll discover that the hardest workers aren't necessarily the greatest time managers, but it doesn't imply you should work less hard. Following good time management methods include implementing measures that maximize the available hours of the day into your daily, weekly, and monthly routine.

Let's look at 12 of these tactics to discover how you might increase your productivity without having to work extra overtime at the workplace.

1. Understand You're Not Perfect

The truth that they are not flawless is one of the hardest things for many individuals to accept. They believe that since they are taking every precaution and prepared for every imaginable eventuality, nothing will go wrong. Unfortunately, everyone with this perspective will face a harsh reality check at some time.

Take a minute right now to recognize that it is OK to make errors and be imperfect. Keep this in mind as you work to improve your time management abilities, remembering that even the best-laid plans may alter or fail. Instead of feeling defeated by these situations, these beliefs will provide avenues for you to progress.

2. Plan Out Each Day

Even if plans alter, this does not imply you should not make any preparations at all. There are various methods to accomplish this, so it may take some time to figure out what works best for you. Many individuals find it beneficial to spend a few minutes each night before bed planning their day's activities.

3. Prioritize Your Daily, Weekly, & Monthly Tasks

You should establish the priorities for the following days, weeks, and even months as part of your planning meetings. Keeping track of upcoming chores will help you to distribute your workload in such a manner that you are not overburdened or anxious. You'll be able to create a more disciplined routine for your daily objectives and stay busy all week.

4. Use Time Management Tools

Speaking of to-do lists, one of the finest ways to manage your time more effectively is to use as many tools as required to support your stance. There are millions of computer applications and smartphone apps available for free download to make your life simpler. Adding just one time management tool to your arsenal may save you hours of labour each week.

5. Do Not Multitask

Did you know that multitasking might reduce your understanding and overall intellect by up to 11%? Attempting to accomplish more than one project at a time might have disastrous consequences for both you and others around you. And for those who don't think it's so horrible, consider earning 11% less each year than you do now.

6. Determine Your Productive Times

Do you prefer the morning or the evening, or do you fall somewhere in between? These kinds of inquiries may often aid your time management tactics by determining when you're most effective throughout the day.

A person who can bounce out of bed wide-eyed and bushy-tailed a minute before their alarm goes off will most likely be able to get more work done in the early hours of the day. A night owl, on the other hand, may move more slowly when they wake up and need some time to get back into their typical work routine. Those folks frequently have a greater degree of productivity in the afternoon.

7. Remove Distractions

What is the significance of time management? Because the world is full of red herrings waiting to divert your attention away from your job and other obligations. Some of the most common workplace distractions are:

- Smartphones
- Social Media
- Internet
- Email
- Co-workers
- Meetings (Unless they are powerful and fruitful)

8. Use a Timer

As strange as it may seem, utilizing a timer may be one of the most effective time management tools available. Setting a timer may help you remember to take breaks, establish time limitations, and even become more productive. Breaks are an important component of every workday since they allow you to move away from your desk and clear your thoughts for a brief period before returning to work.

9. Split Large Projects into Pieces

Have you ever looked at a project and wanted to flee because it seemed to be too intricate and difficult? You may want to check into the specifics. Breaking down huge milestones and deadlines into smaller side tasks and goals is a terrific approach for managing your time on a large project.

10. Learn to Say "No" More Often

Have you ever watched the Jim Carrey film "Yes Man"? The comedy's core plot revolves around a pessimistic banker who chooses to say "yes" to everything after attending a positivity seminar. While it leads to some amusing scenarios, the main character soon understands that being overly eager to achieve anything may lead to significant problems.

The fundamental Chapter of the tale is to avoid becoming the office's "yes guy" or "yes lady." If you often find yourself overworked or weighed down by too many duties, you may need to start saying "no" when someone asks you to assist them. This may open up a world of possibilities for you to better manage your time and increase the value of your job.

12. Recharge Your Batteries

Some may consider this the most important of all time management tactics for your overall performance and sanity. So many industries throughout the globe are always in combat mode, facing the next crisis or addressing the next issue on the agenda. But, in the middle of all the commotion, you should always make time to sit back and relax.

Taking a break from your daily grind to relax your mind and body may help you remain focused and enthusiastic when you return to your desk, warehouse, or construction site.

11. Delegate Work When You Can

When you are extremely busy, you should seek possibilities to outsource your job, which is similar to the previous two-time management strategies. If you are given a task with a deadline that you will not be able to meet on your own, share the burden with your team and work together to complete it.

Chapter 2.4: How to Organize and Manage Your Time

Your day, like everyone else's, is just twenty-four hours long. Nonetheless, some individuals seem to be able to do more than others. What is their secret? Time management refers to how you plan, prioritize, and create daily. You cannot manufacture more time, but effective time management will make you happier, healthier, and more productive.

Time management is highly dependent on your specific personal circumstances, but a few broad guidelines may help you better organize your life and profession, considerably boosting your time management abilities—regardless of what's on your plate.

1. See the big picture

You've heard the adage; *they couldn't see the forest for the trees*? When you're chaotic and drowning in information, it's practically hard to be productive. What you need is a bird's-eye perspective of your whole calendar and task, as well as a clear grasp of the broad picture. Only with a clear view of the big picture can you efficiently dig down into the details and get things done.

2. Identify priorities early

Priorities are an excellent strategy to guarantee a productive day. You must understand what activities must be completed first and why, as well as a broad idea of which jobs will be completed and when. That should happen before your day begins, with an honest evaluation of what needs to be done and how long it will take.

You should explicitly strive to:

- **Consolidate** Put all of your chores on one list and categories them by month, week, or day.

- **Separate** duties of higher priority from those of lesser importance and

- **Build** them into your day by handling the most critical things first and leaving the less important ones for last.

3. Centralize information

Accessibility is essential for good time management; time spent looking for information is lost time. Consolidate all of your notes, tasks, and schedules in one spot to make your life simpler. You'll be able to step back and receive a clear, unified, big-picture perspective of your issue, as well as better prioritize your to-dos—and you won't waste time looking for crucial information.

The more easily you can get the knowledge you need, the more quickly you can act on it. If you have to frequently switch between applications to get the information you need, it will harm your time management and create a lot of irritation.

4. Set deadlines—and stick to them

The most critical aspect of every work is the deadline, whether it is self-imposed or enforced. Deadlines provide you with a schedule and an indication of how much time you'll need to dedicate to each work.

Many individuals plan their days by making a checklist and checking off each job as they finish it. Unfortunately, this attitude is not conducive to effective time management and may even be detrimental. Simple lists are seldom prioritized and fail to account for the projected duration of each activity. Rather than relying on to-do lists, organize your work according to deadlines. Remember to plan ahead of time for more time-consuming undertakings.

To improve your task management, follow these four rules:

1. **Make it urgent.** It's simpler to procrastinate when you have all the time in the world to finish a job. Without a feeling of urgency, it's easy to get distracted by less strenuous activities that are typically unrelated to your task. To keep on track and motivated, set an early deadline for yourself.

2. **Make it fit.** The way you manage your time is unique to you, and the chores in your life reflect that. Rather than attempting to push everything into a predefined timetable, arrange your calendar to achieve those things in a manner that works for those patterns.

3. **Make it actionable.** Don't simply take notes on what you need to accomplish. Consider how you will accomplish it and what you will need. Then you're all set to do your work.

4. **Make it meaningful.** The deadline must be respected, and you must be responsible to both yourself and your team.

5. Take smarter breaks

Fear of losing productivity often inhibits individuals from taking necessary breaks. Nonetheless, breaks are not only healthful but also vital for productive working. They operate best when the following conditions are met:

- A break should be spent doing something completely different from what you were doing before.

- It should keep you in a job-related mindset, enabling you to return to work swiftly.

- Any break is beneficial, as long as it is taken when you need it.

Well-planned breaks every 45-90 minutes have been shown to improve health. When the break is finished, they create a feeling of well-being by lowering tension and helping you to better concentrate on your task.

Time to get organized

Work patterns driven by pandemics, such as remote and hybrid working arrangements, have created havoc on how individuals manage their time, and failing to achieve a good work-life balance might mean tragedy. Procrastination, failure to accomplish objectives, and even burnout may emerge from problems in one area fast cascading into the other.

It's a common struggle: you want to be productive at work and home, yet the expectations, deadlines, and diversions never seem to stop. You need to get more done in less time while being productive, but how?

Tasks + Notes cooperate to help you get to your objectives quicker, narrowing the gap between what you need to accomplish and the information you need to do.

Calendar + Notes + Tasks turbocharges your sessions, reducing preparation time with all the information you need at the push of a button

Home + Notes + Calendar + Tasks Organize your day in a dashboard that combines what you need to know with what you need to accomplish. Your most essential notes, most pressing tasks, and most recent schedule are all displayed in a single integrated view. Rather than being overwhelmed by knowledge, make it work for you.

Making the best use of your time and doing the right thing at the appropriate time is what time management entails. Smart time management allows you to be more productive and achieve progress in several aspects of your life while keeping stress and energy levels under control. Knowing the worth of your time means you are seldom overloaded and can enjoy every job or life moment to the utmost.

Chapter 2.5: Time Management for Beginners

If you're new to time management, you're undoubtedly wondering, "Where do I start?"

You may be struggling with an overwhelming list of tasks to do. Or maybe you just want extra time in your day.

Whatever your scenario, you are undoubtedly concerned about time management adding to your workload.

However, the finest productivity tools should reduce your burden rather than increase it.

Refrain from implementing sophisticated time management systems or technologies. You don't need pricey software or equipment to get started.

Instead, small habits and efforts may have a significant impact on your activities.

Here are 10 Top Time Management Tips for Beginners:

1. **Have the Right Tools** – You must have the proper tools for the task. This applies to time management as well as most other aspects of life. Take the time to put together your time management tools.

2. **Keep It Simple** – Keep your time management system as basic as feasible. The power of one. The most basic tools are accessible.

3. **Don't Spend a Lot of Money on Technology** – You do not need any pricey software or equipment. Yes, there are fantastic applications to aid you, but if you're just starting, the built-in apps on your phone are typically sufficient. A pad of paper, for example, may be more effective than complicated equipment.

4. **Clean Workspace** – Less clutter means more space for productivity. Clear away the clutter on your desk to make more room for serious work.

5. **Make a List** – It's amazing how many people go through their days without making a list of what they need to accomplish. Making a list allows you to keep track of all the items on your to-do list. It also frees up your mind to focus on the task at hand.

6. **Plan Your Day** – A little forethought may save you a lot of time later in the day. Even 5 minutes of checking your schedule and to-do list can save you a lot of tension and friction in your life.

7. **Start Early** – The early bird gets the worm. If you're just getting started with time management, start early... before the rest of the world. Early morning hours may be some of the most productive, allowing you to do your most critical tasks before others are up.

8. **Make Appointments with Your Work** – Even little chores need time allocation. Don't allow the events of the day to push your to-do list to the side. Schedule appointments on your calendar for your most critical chores instead.

9. **Control Your Technology** – Technology may be a fantastic tool for helping you get more work done. It may, however, distract you and take your time. Remember that your phone and other electronics are there for your convenience, not for the convenience of others. Turn off your alerts, and don't answer your phone if you're busy.

10. **Practice Saying No** – You can't do everything. Nobody can. Make difficult decisions about how you will spend your time.

Chapter 2.6: How to Ensure Productivity Through Time Management

Managing your time well can do wonders for your job - you'll be able to do everything on time, limit your workload, and stay productive without hurrying or feeling frustrated.

However, good time management may be tough; according to one report, individuals spend just 2 hours and 53 minutes being productive during work hours.

However, there are strategies to increase these figures and guarantee that you procrastinate less while still getting more work done.

Here are eight basic time management ideas to help you conquer productivity and simplify your work routine.

1. Identify Your Most Productive Time

Everyone has a most productive time of day that is dictated by their Circadian rhythms - internal clocks that control when you do particular things best.

By following your internal clock, you become more effective in your job since you are doing it when you are most awake, focused, and energetic.

Consider your present routines and your effectiveness in doing them before deciding on your productivity peak hours.

Do you start working first thing in the morning but struggle to focus, so you waste hours procrastinating? If this is the case, early mornings are not the greatest time to do your most critical job, and you should schedule it for later in the day.

Experiment with tracking the time you spend on the same tasks at various times of the day using a time management tool to determine your most productive period.

When you review your findings afterwards, you may discover that, for the same work, it takes you:

1. 3 hours in the morning
2. 2 hours around noon
3. and 1.5 hours in the late afternoon

This demonstrates that late afternoon is the time when you do the highest quality work, and it is also when you should always handle your most critical chores. You should also save less important chores for your less productive hours, such as emails or meetings.

2. Use A Time Management App

The greatest way to improve your time management is to keep track of how you spend it. You should determine how long it takes you to complete a job and if some activities take longer than expected.

It allows you to measure the time you spend on tasks, produce reports that highlight your outcomes, and pinpoint where you waste time.

As an experiment, you may use the time management tool to measure how much time you spend on each of your tasks at work throughout the day:

1. your assignments and projects
2. social media
3. the Internet
4. inbox management
5. breaks
6. meetings
7. phone calls

When you write a report and review your findings, you may learn that you spent:

1. 45 minutes on social media
2. 1 hour on managing your inbox
3. 30 minutes on an irrelevant phone call

In the end, that's 2 hours and 15 minutes you could have spent doing something more productive.

Next time, try to devote more time to your most essential tasks. By utilising your time clock software to measure time regularly, you'll always have significant data revealing whether and where your routine needs to be improved.

3. Prioritize tasks

Not all tasks are created equal, and you should prioritise them depending on their significance before tackling them in that order.

To begin, make daily to-do lists and fill them with chores for the following day. This way, you won't lose time just before starting your workday thinking about what you need to accomplish.

Make these lists the night before so you don't have to worry about them in the morning when you should be concerned about other things.

Make a list of the activities in order of significance, with the most essential tasks at the top and the least important ones at the bottom.

Remember that investing all of your efforts into one endeavour may help you more than focusing on five separate projects at the same time. This is known as the Pareto Principle. If you put 20% of your efforts in the appropriate direction, you will get 80% of your intended objectives.

For example, if you're a programmer addressing bugs, try to fix 20% of all flaws that will solve 80% of your program's problems.

If there are any items on your to-do list that aren't urgent or vital, assign them to others or remove them entirely. This will save you a lot of time and enable you to focus on your objectives more.

4. Schedule tasks

Once you've organized all of your to-do lists and items, and identified your most critical chores, you may assign them to certain days of the week and times of the day.

It's advisable to schedule time for each thing on your daily to-do list and note it in your calendar - use Google Calendar or a similar program for this. In the calendar, arrange all of your daily to-do items and mark their start and finish timings.

The end times may function as deadlines, which can help keep you on track - you'll know how much time you have left before you have to complete a task, so you'll be motivated to stay focused on it to beat the clock.

You might prioritize the tasks by assigning your initial working hours to the most critical ones. Alternatively, you might schedule this work at your most productive time of day.

Make time for breaks and unscheduled activities; you never know when you'll need to re-arrange priorities when something unexpected comes up.

For the greatest results, arrange comparable activities together in your calendar and work on them sequentially.

5. Address distractions

Distractions occur in many kinds and sizes, and it is critical to handle them: social media, the Internet, your phone, interruptions, and background sounds are all major sources of distraction.

A website blocker is the greatest approach to remove social media and other time-wasting websites during work hours. There are different versions for different devices, but most function on the same principle: you add the URL links of distracting websites to a blacklist and set the time limit for how long you won't be able to access them.

If you place your phone somewhere out of reach during work hours, such as in a separate room, it will be more difficult for you to continue checking it or otherwise be distracted by it.

Use time management software to obtain a clear picture of how much time you spend on social media and other distractions, as well as to see how much time you can save.

When working in an open workplace, headphones may be used to block out much of the surrounding noise. You may use a noise generator or appropriate music. According to one Middle Tennessee State University research, instrumentals boost focus and performance.

You may also utilize headphones to signal that you are working so that your coworkers do not bother you during this time.

After you've eliminated all distractions, you'll be able to focus on your task without worrying about anything breaking your attention.

6. Work while waiting or commuting

Waiting at the dentist or driving to work may seem to be time wasted, but you may utilise it to enhance your job.

You probably bring your phone, tablet, or even a laptop with you everywhere you go so you can work during long waits and commutes.

Simply choose less important jobs that you can do with fewer resources and go to work. You may, for example, utilize this time to respond to emails, evaluate proposals, and undertake basic research for your next project.

Whatever you choose to accomplish, you will reduce the task that greets you in the workplace, saving you time in the long run.

7. Take breaks

Breaks may seem to be counterproductive in your quest to do more in less time, but they help you concentrate by allowing you to recharge when you're fatigued and distracted.

If you kept working until you finished a job, you would risk burnout from overwork. You also risk rushing an assignment or project, which might lead to time-consuming rewrites and modifications later on.

According to one University of Illinois study, taking short breaks helps you concentrate. Furthermore, a Florida State University study says that humans can only be productive for 90 minutes at a time before needing to take a break.

You may pick how much time you want to spend on breaks:

1. first, break - 5 minutes to make a cup of tea
2. second break - 15 minutes to meditate and relax.
3. third break - 10 minutes for a jog to clear your mindset

The main thing is to adjust your break time based on how tired you are and how long you believe you'll need before you can continue.

You'll feel energetic and renewed after the break, and you'll be more inclined to concentrate on the work at hand.

8. Organize your workspace

Knowing where all of your key files, folders, and documents are can save you a lot of time searching for them.

Always keep critical papers close at hand, whether in drawers or properly arranged on your desk. Sort everything by category and subject, and store similar materials together, such as notes, critical documentation, books, and manuals relevant to your profession.

If you know you'll need a certain collection of papers the next day, place them on your table the day before.

Use the following methods on your laptop or desktop computer:

1. arrange and organize relevant items into folders
2. Delete the files and folders you no longer need at the end of the week or month.
3. Alternatively, establish an "Archive" folder and save any documents that you no longer actively work on but want to save in there.

You'll feel more in charge of what you do if you organize your paperwork, and you'll spend less time preparing for events.

CHAPTER 3: TIME MANAGEMENT FOR DIFFERENT PERSONNEL

Chapter 3.1: Time Management for Entrepreneurs

As an entrepreneur, you are in charge of every element of your company. You have a lot on your plate, from developing and implementing plans to chairing meetings, managing your personnel, and meeting new customers.

Work pressure may sometimes get so intense that you feel overwhelmed. You begin to believe that you will never be able to perform your chores successfully and on time. Such sentiments impair your productivity and efficiency. As a consequence, your company begins to suffer. The good news is that you can completely control your work schedule by improving your time management abilities.

Efficient time management is one of the most crucial abilities for busy entrepreneurs to have to keep their companies running smoothly. No matter how hectic your schedule is, as the company owner, you must devote the appropriate amount of time to each activity.

The issue is that not everyone understands how to effectively manage their time. That's why I've compiled a list of three of my favourite time management tricks to help you enhance the way you arrange and complete your activities.

Let's have a look at them.

1. Use technology to save time.

Have you thought of leveraging technology to save time? My favourite way to save time in my hectic schedule is to use productivity tools. Technology has improved to the point that tasks may now be completed almost half the time and with twice the efficiency.

Although certain duties cannot be entrusted to the machines, there are several tasks that the machines can do. For example, various jobs must be completed daily. Because such tasks do not need much attention and can be handled without human assistance, why not automate them? This is an excellent choice for chores such as social media posting, email answers, appointment reminders, and so on. This will not only save you time, but it will also assist you to be more productive.

2. Set time limits.

As an entrepreneur, you may have multiple meetings to attend as well as several other things to do throughout the day. But bear in mind that a day only has 24 hours. So don't allow any unforeseen meetings, teleconferences, or other demands to take up more of your time.

However, you may encounter problems that cannot be avoided. Setting a hard stop time is a smart way to manage time when such unanticipated occurrences occur. Make a point of not spending more than 20 minutes on unexpected meetings or 10 minutes on unscheduled calls. That way, you get your work done without having to work too hard to fit it into your schedule.

3. Concentrate on one activity at a time.

The concept of multitasking is not new. You may believe that doing numerous things at once allows you to get more done, but the fact is that it reduces your productivity and wastes a lot of time.

Focusing on one job at a time is the most effective strategy to do more tasks. As a result, your task will be completed sooner. And once completed, you may effortlessly turn your attention to your next task. Having your complete concentration on one activity increases efficiency, which increases production.

One of the most critical skills for businesses is effective time management. But keep in mind that effective time management entails not just managing your time more efficiently, but also managing it strategically to get more work done.

Chapter 3.2: Time Management for Single Moms

It is difficult to raise a kid on your own. As a single mother, you are solely responsible for all elements of day-to-day care. If you are one of those who are battling to find quality time, keep reading to learn time management ideas for single working mothers. Being a single mother may cause additional stress, exhaustion, and strain. There never seems to be enough time in the day to get everything done. There is an endless to-do list with less time to do it. You may feel overwhelmed and delayed at times when your to-do list becomes longer and longer.

Time management for single mothers varies greatly from that of married mothers. Because you are on your own, the tasks may continue. Don't let that emotion consume you; here are some simple time management suggestions for single parents.

Time Management Tips For Single-Working Moms

1. Consider Working for a Parent-Friendly Company.

It's difficult to find flexible employment, but it's doable if you look. Employers are more flexible and tolerant of single working parents these days, considering the plight of mothers, particularly single mothers who work full-time.

2. Encourage Your Children to Clean Up the Mess

The basic concept is to encourage your children to tidy up while also recognizing their achievements. This will eventually save you a significant amount of time. Make the 'cleaning the room' duty more enjoyable for them and praise them for their efforts. They will like the jobs you set them in this manner.

3. Let Go The Perfection

Because the notion of perfection does not exist in parenting, there is no purpose in pushing it too much. Instead of forcing yourself to clean the home or working hard to become a supermom or obtain that 'ideal' body, try to make better use of your time.

4. List Your Things According To The Priorities

It's a frequent mind process to put off doing things we don't want to do. However, we fail to remove the unneeded items from the list. Get it done and check it off your list; this will help you get through the much simpler duties later in the day or week.

5. Prepare Everything A Day In Advance

Prepare for the following day ahead of time to avoid being late. If your children bring lunch to school, prepare their meals the night before. Place everything they'll need near the door at night so they can simply grab and go when it's time to go to daycare/school.

6. Have Your Groceries Delivered

Shopping for food takes an unusual amount of time. After a hard day at work, the last thing you want to do is go grocery shopping. Signing up for an online grocery delivery service will save you time and bother. Some firms even provide discounts for repeat customers. Don't forget to enlist the assistance of your children in putting the goods away.

7. Set Attainable Daily Goals

What's the purpose of making a list of impossible goals? We are not superheroes, and we should not pretend to be. Make your everyday objectives realistic and attainable. Remember that you can always accomplish more if you have the time, so prepare ahead of time.

Chapter 3.3: Time Management for Writers

There is no one-size-fits-all guidance sheet for time management, but a good beginning point is to consider if your present activity is what you need to accomplish the goal you've set for yourself.

Using the example of a first-time author who wishes to complete their first work, the objective for this individual will be to devote as much writing time as feasible.

That's the overall picture of time management; what about the details? What about strategies and hacks?

The truth is that your details will be unique to your aims and circumstances, but there are some suggestions I can provide.

Take the ones that work for you, make any necessary changes, and toss the others.

1. Get your words down first

This is the most typical piece of time management advice I provide to the authors with whom I collaborate. Make writing your priority when you wake up.

Having your thoughts written down before the rest of the world begins placing demands on you is a really powerful sensation.

2. Use your day job downtime

The majority of individuals are not working nonstop throughout the day. They're sneaking Facebook breaks or squandering time gossiping with colleagues.

And here's the thing: your employer is well aware of this. Plan your downtime intelligently and utilize it as pockets of time to monitor your social media, conduct research, create your email newsletter, and more, as long as your supervisor hasn't raised concerns about your productivity levels or the amount of time you're zoning out while on the clock.

3. Batch similar activities

Take advantage of the momentum you'll get while working on a certain task by performing more of it at once.

You may record many podcast episodes on the same day, plan out a month's worth of social media, plan out a year's worth of content ideas, or plan out various email exchanges or promotions for the future months.

4. Say no

You'll probably have to start saying no to other things to say yes to the objectives you want to attain. It's all right. And, as Oprah says, "no" is a whole phrase.

5. Delegate

What are you doing now that someone else could do? Remember that time saved in your personal life may free up time for writing, so make sure that the individuals you live with are completing their fair part of household management tasks.

6. Accept your limitations

There will be aspects of your writing company that fall outside of your skill set. I wouldn't know where to begin with the cover design. Maybe you can accomplish that, but you don't know how to format your books.

Accept that spending a disproportionate amount of time for a mediocre outcome does not make sense from a time management standpoint if you are attempting to achieve anything. Can you hire someone to do it? If not, can you barter or exchange talents or services?

7. Limit distractions

Even if you sell everything and relocate to a lonely Scottish island, you'll never be fully free of distractions. You may, however, restrict them.

First, identify them. Which distractions have the most impact on you? Is it your family, the internet, or group chat? How do you get rid of them?

8. Change your smartphone notification settings

Two-thirds of individuals never adjust their smartphone's notification settings, which means they're continually distracted by updates from dozens of applications throughout the day.

If this is you, go to your settings and turn off all non-urgent alerts. For instance, I only get push alerts for text messages, WhatsApp messages, and phone calls.

9. Check your email less

You probably check your email more than you should. If you feel especially tethered to your inbox because you need to be reachable for customers or coworkers, establish an autoreply that says something like, "I check email twice a day, at 10 a.m. and 3 p.m. If your email is time-sensitive and cannot wait until then, please contact me at ."

In my experience, individuals who follow up on an email with a call do so when you take more than five minutes to respond, therefore this autoreply will not significantly boost the number of calls you get.

Chapter 3.4: Time Management for High School Students

Time management enables you to fulfil all of your tasks within a certain time frame. It will assist you in organizing your life, which may be challenging throughout the school year.

When you begin managing your time, you will notice improved grades, more productivity, and, eventually, a better attitude!

These recommendations are for all my lazy students who want to get out of bed and not watch Netflix all day! Once you're acclimated to it, the transformation will feel fantastic, and you'll never want to go back.

I understand that high school may be hectic. That is why I want you to put these time management methods into action and give yourself more time to accomplish the things you like.

Let us begin with one of the most crucial time management strategies for high school students...

Have a Schedule

I'm sure you saw that coming, but it's necessary!

The best approach to keep track of everything is to create a timetable in which you can insert your to-do list into particular time intervals.

Monthly, weekly, and daily planners are highly beneficial for keeping track of priorities (which will be discussed soon).

The most crucial component of managing academics and personal life is sticking to your timetable.

Make a practice of taking down notes, odd thoughts, and ideas as you go about your day in your calendar.

You should think of it as your second brain, so you don't have to clutter up your first one!

Prioritize Your To-Do List

Writing down your to-do list is a good start, but prioritizing it is much better. Here's how to go about it:

1. Go through your schedule for the day.
2. Organize comparable jobs together (the time it takes to complete, similar subject, etc.)
3. You should number the jobs in the order you wish to finish them.
4. Begin with a simpler activity at the start of each day (this helps reduce feeling overwhelmed and jump-start your productivity)

Even when I had my to-do list written down, I used to get discouraged when I knew there was a lot to accomplish the following day. That emotion has gone away now that I've prioritized the list.

If you have the same sense, you may be failing to prioritize your time. Give it a go!

Have Long Term and Short-Term Goals

Having both long-term and short-term objectives can help you finish things more quickly and effectively.

Long-term objectives should range from one week to one semester. Short-term objectives should be set within a week, but generally within 1-2 days.

Things become clearer when you organize your time in this manner. You'll know precisely what you need to accomplish and how much time you have to complete it.

Once you've established your long-term objectives, all you have to do is break them down into weekly, daily, or even hourly chores.

Those duties are now your short-term objectives. If you accomplish chores early, take on a little job here and there to finish everything ahead of schedule.

Reward Yourself

Rewarding oneself is a terrific motivation to stick to your objectives.

Humans are hardwired to perform better in activities that reward them. That is why we work hard for A's, train hard for gold medals, and study hard for raises.

When it comes to time management advice for students, these incentives may be as easy as giving yourself a piece of candy after completing your daily responsibilities.

Get in the Habit of Using Reminders

Although I do not recommend using technology to organize your day, setting reminders on your phone may be a stress-free method to manage your time.

You should still write down your objectives in a calendar, but reminders may help you remember when it's time to finish them.

For example, if you don't have your planner and you just left class, your phone might remind you to jot down the homework you were given or to start preparing for a test.

Reminders are your backup planner for items you may forget.

Avoid Distractions When Studying

This is perhaps one of the most difficult time management techniques for high school students to master.

We like diversions. When we don't want to perform a hard job, we enjoy procrastination.

Here's what I propose you start doing right now...

- Turn off your phone for chores that require more than 30 minutes.
- Set your computer to full-screen mode to prevent opening more tabs.
- Only listen to music that is intended to help you concentrate (songs without lyrics)
- Study on an empty stomach, with water nearby.

Write down the four bullet points above and tape them to the wall in front of your workstation so you don't forget!

We become sidetracked by everything and everything, so block them out for good while you're studying.

How to Make Your Studying Time More Effective

A specific formula was developed for the most effective studying strategy. I exclusively use this approach now, and it works well!

It's known as the Pomodoro Technique, and here is how it works:

1. Work for 25 minutes
2. Take a 5-minute break
3. Repeat 4 times
4. After the 4th cycle, take a longer 30-minute break

This strategy provides incredible memory retention and will eventually save you time in the long run!

To remain on track, I suggest setting a timer for the 25-minute sessions. Instead of using your phone during breaks, go get some water or food

Multitasking Will Ruin Results

I can't speak for everyone since some folks can make it work. However, if you're considering multitasking, I'd advise against it.

Getting numerous tasks done at the same time statistically does not make sense if you want to be 100% efficient.

It's almost hard to devote your complete attention to two projects at the same time.

Furthermore, all of the other time management ideas for high school students are sufficient to eliminate the need to multitask in the first place. Use the other suggestions to make high school less difficult.

Minimize Deadlines

There is a hypothesis about limiting deadlines that states that we allow ourselves much too much time to finish things, which reduces our productivity.

For example, if you have an essay due in three weeks, reduce the deadline to one week. Furthermore, when you begin writing the essay, allow yourself three hours rather than the whole day.

We can do projects quicker than we believe for whatever reason! This is something to keep in mind if your schedule is very hectic.

The 2-Minute Rule

We have a habit of putting off the most difficult chores until the last.

These duties may include things like scrubbing a bowl after eating from it, doing laundry, writing something down, sending an email to a teacher, and so on.

What the 2-minute rule indicates...

Do something right immediately if it takes 2 minutes or less.

This may be tough for you at first, but as someone who does it all the time now, I can tell you that I feel a lot more organized. Following this guideline has drastically improved my time management (for the better)!

How to Keep Track of the Time Spent on Each Class

The easiest method to arrange your time is to do the following:

1. Create a syllabus overview that includes all of the semester's important deadlines.

2. The outline should be colour coded (use a different colour for every class)

3. Use the time management suggestions on prioritizing listed above to rank the significance of the tasks.
4. Divide your time based on when tasks are due and how long it takes to do them.

Everyone will have a different approach. This strategy has simply worked for my pals and me.

The most crucial thing to remember here is your syllabus due dates. That is your primary goal for correctly dividing the time.

CHAPTER 4: TRACK YOURSELF TO UNDERSTAND YOURSELF BETTER

Chapter 4.1: Control Your Day

How well do you manage your time? Do you go to work believing you've planned everything so that you'll finish in record time, only to find yourself behind schedule at the end of the day? Perhaps it is time to fine-tune your time management abilities and learn how to take charge of your day and enhance productivity.

First things first

The first step in doing this is to identify where your time is going. One of the best methods to achieve this is to record every hour of your day for a week; this will help you see and examine how your workday is spent.

The final analysis

The following findings may surprise or maybe shock you:

- How much time do you spend talking to co-workers?
- How much time do you devote to checking your email?
- Do you spend time on social media?
- How often do co-workers interrupt you?

You will discover how to take charge of your day and enhance productivity by following some of these suggestions:

Plan & prioritize

Make it a habit to spend 15-20 minutes after each week itemizing and prioritizing the jobs and projects that must be done the following week. Set aside the time needed to complete the most critical tasks and refuse any last-minute meetings unless they are required. Help people understand your objectives, especially your boss, and solicit their participation.

Push back the non-essential tasks

A good example of a non-essential chore is cleaning up your email "Inbox." After you've listed and prioritized your tasks, go through them again and rate them from most important to least important on a scale of 1-3. If it has no bearing on anything else important and can be postponed, then put it back on your calendar.

The importance of setting goals

While you may not always have complete control over your day, you may exert as much control as possible by adhering to some of the following guidelines:

1. Set daily objectives for what you want to achieve that day.
2. Schedule a time of day to check and respond to emails; do not check again unless you are waiting for time-sensitive information.
3. Concentrate and avoid multitasking; tackling one thing at a time will allow you to achieve more and boost your overall productivity.
4. Consider how you spend your time regularly. Would you classify the work at hand as "billable," implying that the firm benefits from your efforts, or "non-billable," implying that the duties do not necessarily add to the bottom line?
5. One of the most difficult skills to learn is how to say "no." We're all trying to be polite in the sandbox and assist others. We don't want to look uncooperative or get a poor rating in our reviews. If your productivity is hurting, though, your coworkers will understand if you just say: "I wish I could assist you with that, but I'm currently working on two other projects. Would you want to set aside some time to work on it?" You will most likely gain their respect for your honesty and discipline, and they will look forward to having your undivided attention at the scheduled time.

By incorporating these suggestions into your daily routine, you will find yourself managing your time more efficiently and becoming more disciplined. These are some tried-and-true methods for taking charge of your day and increasing productivity.

Chapter 4.2: Control Your Life

Time is Life

"Life is Time. It is unchangeable and irrevocable. "Wasting your time is wasting your life." At first glance, the book seems to be all about extreme efficiency. It is, however, about making the most of one's life. We don't have a shortage of time, but we don't utilize it properly to attain our greatest objectives so that we don't feel unhappy and out of control.

Control = Freedom and Choice

The central concept of this work is "control." This is not an obsessive control. A balanced control that allows you to get things done while still having fun. Control also implies a decision. You are the one who decides what works and what does not. Time management success is very personal.

Control = Planning

Control begins with preparation. You must arrange your time regularly. "Failing to plan is intending to fail," Lakein argues.

"Drift, drown, or decide," says Lakein another time.

The world and other people are continuously vying for your attention. You must take the initiative to make choices for yourself.

"Planning is bringing the future into the present so you can do something about it now," Lakein says.

Planning is best conceived of as "writing" rather than "thinking," so grab a notepad right now.

Goals

You must have objectives to create suitable priorities for your everyday tasks. Write down your responses to the following questions:

What are my long-term objectives?

How do I want to spend the next three years?

What would I do if I only had six months left to live?

If your responses to the three questions do not closely correspond, you most likely have a problem. Consider why they do not link. Being honest with yourself will make it difficult to manage your time and arrange your life appropriately.

Priorities

The fundamentals of planning are as follows: 1) create a to-do list, and 2) establish priorities. After you've established a list of potential activities, the hard process of ranking them begins. You must consider the criteria by which you prioritize your priorities. Consider your objectives. Is it true that family comes first? Earning money? Fun? The order in which you prioritize them will impact which acts you execute first, which are left for later, and which are never completed.

Rank activities from A to C in order of significance. Then, in each area, rate the activities again, with 1 being the most essential, 2 being the second most important, and so on down the list. The ABCs are related to the person and the circumstance. You make the call. Your responses evolve.

Work on your A-1 aim until it is complete.

Resist the temptation to focus on other, more comfortable objectives, including your A-2 aim. When an A is left undone, do not work on Bs or Cs. Keep the list as visible as possible and work from it.

Scheduling

We are all aware that this is critical, yet it is easier said than done. The world throws things at us, and we must cope with them. Suddenly, it's hours or even years later, and we still haven't finished what we stated was our A-1.

Your A-1 objectives must be scheduled on your calendar. Set aside your finest time for your objectives. When you are at your most productive, work on those objectives. Push busy work and other people's demands to the margins of your calendar.

Doing Nothing

Taking charge of your time does not imply becoming a "Time Nut," as Lakein refers to it. It is important to unwind and do nothing. Do not pack a task into every available minute.

We all need time to unwind, care for ourselves, have fun, and contemplate.

Making the right choices is at the heart of the Lakein technique.

When we can slow down and connect our aspirations with reality, we can make better decisions.

SLOW DOWN when it comes to "decision time."

Making impulsive judgments under time constraints is not beneficial in the long term.

Saying No

Someone will always be dissatisfied with how you spend your time. It is impossible to satisfy everyone. Saying no quickly and politely solves a lot of difficulties.

However, you may have to postpone your A aim to complete someone else's C goal. It might be your spouse or a kid. Determine the degree of your connection with the individual and the repercussions of not assisting them. If a flat "No" is not an option, then dialogue and compromise will be required to assist others while still making time for your A objectives.

The hardest person to say no to is yourself. Leave the Cs with low priority undone. You must fight the temptation to work your way down your to-do list out of internal reluctance or avoidance. Follow through on your objectives and priorities. Group non-emergency requests from others and your low-priority busy work into scheduled "office hours" that don't interfere with your core work.

Be Aware

You will encounter internal opposition to your aspirations. To escape difficult duties, you will engage in escapism. You will have willpower failures.

Slow down and investigate the roots of your resistance.

Is it fear, a misalignment of aims, or over-commitment? Commit to being truthful with yourself. To gain momentum, focus on completing little activities related to your A objectives.

Apply Pareto's 80/20 principle to your outcomes analysis. What is the source of your success? Concentrate on it. Where do you get the most out of your resistance? Remove it at its source.

Recenter yourself as often as possible by asking yourself, "What is the best use of my time right now?"

Acceptance

Nobody is flawless. There is seldom a direct path to success. Take it easy on yourself. "Do your best and consider it a success," Lakein advises.

Chapter 4.3: Positive Routines

In our daily lives, we often find ourselves sliding into habits known as routines. On any given day, many individuals walk their dogs, go to work, clean, exercise, and pay bills. These routine everyday duties may be difficult at times, particularly if you have a mental health condition.

Developing habits may provide comfort and encourage happy sensations. Did you know that scheduling may also help with mental health and good behaviour?

HOW ROUTINES SUPPORT MENTAL HEALTH

Setting a new habit may be difficult, but schedules provide significant advantages to one's mental health. When healthy behaviours are adopted regularly, they may provide long-term advantages.

Routines may help with mental health in the following ways:

- **Increase productivity** - Planning for the day ahead and knowing what's coming up in your schedule assists you to save time and energy that you can put toward other activities.

- **Alleviate stress and anxiety** - Making a routine enables you to develop good habits, which will reduce tension and anxiety in the long term.

- **Create time for things that matter most** - A routine allows you to take control of your day and plan it around what is most important to you.

Completing basic things, no matter how modest, may be pleasant and make you feel good about yourself.

Routines may be useful to other members of your household as well. Routines may be particularly effective if you have a kid with attention deficit hyperactivity disorder (ADHD), a child on the autistic spectrum, or a youngster who suffers from an anxiety problem.

HELPING CHILDREN WITH ADHD THROUGH ROUTINES

Children with attention deficit hyperactivity disorder (ADHD) may difficulty with time management, organization, and remembering things. This might add to the tension of a youngster who is already suffering from anxiety.

Routines and habits may help youngsters build structure and learn how to handle stress in their lives.

Consider the following while developing an ADHD management routine:

- **Set alarms 30 minutes earlier than scheduled** - Mornings may be busy and stressful. Make time for your kid to gradually wake up and begin their day without feeling rushed.

- **Lay out clothes, pack lunches, and create a task list the night before** - This eliminates one step from your daily ritual, allowing you to get your day started on the right foot.

- **Put electronics away each morning to reduce distractions** - Following a timetable and avoiding disruptions keeps everyone on track.

Making a daily schedule and incorporating specific hours when duties should begin and end provides clear advice for both you and your kid. Getting acquainted with your routines and doing them regularly can help you integrate them into your everyday activities.

WHY DO ROUTINES HELP AUTISM SPECTRUM DISORDERS CHILDREN?

Many youngsters with autism spectrum disorders (ASD) exhibit hyperactivity and impulsive behaviour. They may be particularly fond of animals, novels, video games, music, or electrical gadgets. Attachment to items or ideas may manifest itself in recurrent behaviours or the formation of collections.

Structure and regular routines might help children understand what to anticipate and reduce their fear of change. Incorporating a timetable to assist deal with life's unpredictability might help to alleviate this anxiety.

Consider the following suggestions when creating routines for children with autism spectrum disorders:

- **Create consistent schedules** - Children with autism spectrum disorders flourish when they have a stable routine.

- **Make use of visual and audible cues** - Using drawings, labels, and audio cues to create a daily plan may assist children with autism spectrum disorders handle change.

- **Set small realistic goals to build confidence** - Changing anyone's routine may be difficult. Take note of how your youngster reacts to change. You may need to go slowly at first or practice smaller steps over time.

- **Provide alternatives to habits you are trying to limit** - Provide options that may be of interest to them. If your kid enjoys playing with trains, for example, you might read books about them or make illustrations together.

HOW ROUTINES CAN HELP CALM CHILDREN WITH ANXIETY

Anxiety is quite widespread and may affect individuals of all ages, including children. Untreated chronic anxiety may cause problems sleeping, poor energy levels, and even depression.

Routines may aid in the reduction of stress and anxiety. Children and adults will eventually develop a pattern and be able to do activities with greater ease.

Keep the following recommendations in mind to assist your kid to minimize anxiety via routine:

- **Reassess goals and progress frequently** - It's OK to modify a new practice if it doesn't seem right. Changing your child's routine until you discover one that works for you might result in greater results.

- **Add on to an existing routine** - You and your kid may already have a schedule that works for them. Instead of altering everything, incorporate new habits into your routine. This may result in a more efficient and stress-free routine.

- **Allow your child to take breaks** - Do not be too harsh on yourself or your kid if a job takes longer than usual. Instead, take a break and do the rest of the assignment later. Consistency is essential, but so is balance. Knowing when to halt and take a break will help you stay on track with your schedule.

Chapter 4.4: Track Your Daily Habits

Aside from jobs and general activities, you may also keep track of your habits. Building habits entail adhering to a certain pattern or activity, but you must periodically assess your progress. This will allow you to determine if the routine is producing the intended outcomes and whether certain steps need to be modified.

As an example, suppose you've been studying the Finnish language. You haven't missed a single Chapter in six months. However, for some reason, you are dissatisfied with your present level of Finnish knowledge. This input indicates that you must make a change. Perhaps you could complete your study more thoroughly or practise your speaking skills.

The problem is that once you've established certain ground rules for a habit, you must follow them. You should also maintain a log of your daily/weekly activities. When it comes to our Finnish language example, you'll need to track the time you spend studying the language.

The habit tracker and its operation

Using a habit tracker is one of the most practical methods to assess your behaviours. James Clear discusses the fundamental objective of this strategy in his book Atomic Habits.

"A habit tracker is a simple tool for determining whether or not you followed through on a behaviour."

The following is how to utilize a habit tracker:

- **Bring a notepad and a calendar, or use Google Sheets/Excel.**
- **Then, write down all your monthly habits.** For example, your November habits may include reading, working out, learning Finnish, and doing yoga.
- **When you complete a habit, place a check mark,** an X symbol, or any other symbol next to it.

You may choose the days for each habit, for example:

- Monday, Wednesday, and Friday – workout,
- Tuesday and Thursday – learning Finnish,
- Saturday and Sunday – yoga
- Every day – reading.

Here's an example of completing all of your habits in the first week of November.

November 2020

First week	Monday	Tuesday	Wednesday	Thursday	Friday	Saturday	Sunday
Reading	✓	✓	✓	✓	✓	✓	✓
Workout	✓		✓		✓		
Learning Finnish		✓		✓			
Yoga						✓	✓

As you can see, your monthly routines may be separated into identical weekly programs. This strategy, in reality, corresponds to the routines and habits of highly productive individuals. For example, Twitter and Square CEO Jack Dorsey has a distinct regimen for each day of the week. So, Mondays are for managing his businesses, Tuesdays are for product development, and so on.

If you follow this rule, you'll have a month full of marked boxes. This will undoubtedly enhance your motivation. Furthermore, after the first month, you will be able to change the frequency of particular behaviours as required. For example, if you like yoga and find it helps you relax, you may practice it three times a week rather than two.

What behaviours can you quantify?

Clear advocates the Two-Minute Rule in the aforementioned book. This involves beginning with tiny behaviours. Small habits are defined as acts that may be completed in two minutes or less.

Here are some examples of little habits you may develop daily:

- One page from your favourite book
- In the morning, spend one minute meditating.
- One minute of push-ups or stretching
- At the appointed hour, get up and go to bed.
- The optimal time to water your plants is in the afternoon.

Aside from that, you may track health-related behaviours such as:

- How much coffee do you drink every day?
- How much water do you drink each day?
- Whether you consume enough amount of veggies and fruits.
- You can also monitor your protein, carbohydrate, and fat consumption for more thorough nutrition information.

What about the activities you'd prefer to avoid or undertake less frequently? Clear refers to them as avoidance behaviours. In general, these acts are detrimental to your health, money, or productivity. Here are a few such examples:

- Avoiding alcohol, coffee, and sweets.
- Smoking cessation.
- Spending less time in front of the computer or television (outside your work hours).
- Less money is spent on the internet shopping.

As a result, just as you may track the behaviours you want to develop, you can also track the ones you want to avoid.

How do you become acclimated to monitoring your habits?

Even maintaining a record of your routines is a habit you should develop. If you've never monitored your regimen before, here are a few pointers to get you started:

- **As soon as you finish the habit, fill out the habit tracker.** This way, you won't forget to record your daily successes.
- **Keep it simple.** When you have completed the desired habit, just mark the box with the habit's name. You are under no obligation to supply any further information. Keep your habit tracker available as well, so you can simply locate it and fill it out.

Finally, if you stop a habit, try not to repeat it the next day. You undoubtedly have good reasons for missing a routine once, but make sure you get back on schedule the next day.

Chapter 4.5: Track Your Goals

SMART objectives assist people in planning and achieving goals within an acceptable time limit. It may also aid in the improvement of time management in professional contexts such as school and the workplace. If you want to effectively manage your time, SMART goals may give direction for your aims and assist you in creating practical measures to attain those goals. In this post, we will define a SMART objective, describe its advantages, show how to establish SMART goals for time management, and provide examples of SMART goals for time management.

What is a SMART goal?

A SMART goal is an acronym that stands for specified, measurable, achievable, relevant, and time-bound objectives. The objective of developing a SMART goal is to help you utilize your time and resources more effectively while beginning and finishing a project. Consider the following purposes of a SMART objective when you design your own:

- **Specific:** Your objective is clear and concise. It concentrates on one particular area where you want to improve.
- **Measurable:** To assess if you reach your objective, there is a quantitative technique to measure your progress throughout the goal.
- **Attainable:** The aim is achievable. With the necessary resources and talents, you can do it in a respectable length of time.
- **Relevant:** Whether it's a corporate or personal objective, the goal you set has an impact on several elements of your life.

- **Time-Based:** You have set a deadline for yourself to fulfil the objective.

The Advantages of Setting SMART Goals for Time Management

Setting SMART objectives for time management may be advantageous for a variety of reasons. As you develop your time management abilities, you will be able to discern which areas want to work on and concentrate on rectifying them. Among the advantages are:

- Keeping track of your progress during the project
- Increasing productivity and efficiency
- Learning how to prevent procrastinating
- Increasing project possibilities

How to create and reach SMART goals for time management

Here are seven strategies to help you develop and achieve SMART objectives to improve your overall time management:

1. Plan your SMART goal

Using SMART objectives to enhance your time management skills is a wonderful method to add structure to your day since you can clearly outline your goals and adhere to the format to achieve them on time. To help you design a SMART goal for time management, consider answering the following questions:

- **Specific:** What am I hoping to achieve?
- **Measurable:** How will I know when I've reached my goal? What factors can be measured?
- **Attainable:** Is this objective attainable given my abilities, finances, and the amount of work I have to do?
- **Relevant:** What is the relationship between this aim and my broader priorities?

- **Time-based:** When do I intend to finish this task?

2. Create a list

After you've established your SMART objective, try making a list to help you focus on the actions you need to perform to meet your deadline. For example, if the deadline for your goal is in a month, you may develop a step-by-step list with bigger weekly targets to assist you to manage each stage of the process.

Then, for each week, make a list of smaller, more reachable objectives to assist you to accomplish the overarching goal. To aid with time management, make a list of daily chores that must be performed the next day after each day. Because you've previously scheduled your tasks, the list may help you stay focused as you start your day.

3. Block time on your schedule

After you've made your lists, you may utilize a tool to block time in your daily routine. Blocking time may help you stay focused on your activities throughout the day and protect you from getting sidetracked by other chores. It's a useful tool since you can arrange jobs into particular periods using the list you made. You may opt to prioritize the more difficult chores at the start of your day and leave the less complex ones for the finish.

4. Delegate tasks

Delegate chores to others at work whenever feasible. This may demonstrate to your colleagues that you see them as vital and that you trust them. It also enables you to harness the talents and abilities of others to assist you to complete the tasks at hand. Delegating jobs to others may minimize your stress and enable you to be more productive while doing other chores like handling customer concerns or filing performance reports.

5. Take breaks

Setting aside time for breaks during the day is an essential element of time management. To prevent job-related weariness, it is essential to devote time to pursuits other than work. Consider scheduling time-specific breaks outside of lunch that allows you to concentrate on things unrelated to work. Have a snack, go for a little stroll, or check your phone. Whatever you choose, taking a vacation from purely job-related chores is helpful to the quality of your work.

6. Eliminate distractions

It's easy to get sidetracked at work, so strive to eliminate any distractions that may prevent you from finishing a job on time. Cell phones, reading irrelevant emails, having unconnected chats with coworkers, or streaming music or films in the background are all common distractions.

When these distractions are removed, it is typically much simpler to concentrate on each specific activity. Setting limits and avoiding distractions at work might help you become more productive and successful.

7. Concentrate on one activity at a time.

Many individuals strive to multitask to accomplish things during the workday, but concentrating on one item at a time helps you to concentrate totally on that activity. Devoting all of your attention and energy to one work at a time often increases overall speed and provides better quality output than concentrating on numerous projects at once.

Chapter 5: Work on Personal Development

Chapter 5.1: Positive Mentality

To succeed in achieving any objective, you must first think that you can do so.

It is not enough to just practice if you want to be excellent at football, it will undoubtedly assist.

If you are continuously informed that your abilities are inadequate, you will almost certainly fail. You must provide excellent support and have a positive attitude.

Positive mindset

If you take a penalty kick but have no clue where you're going to place it until you kick the ball, you're going to have to depend on luck to succeed. You'll be more likely to strike the proper location if you picture where you're going to kick it. This strategy connects with your subconscious and encourages what you want to achieve.

Simply imagining the event without thinking about it seems to assist your subconscious mind create decisions that help you attain it.

The act of believing in one's accomplishment seems to reduce the dread of failure that causes uncertainty, stress, and bodily changes.

Attitudes and beliefs

Success in reaching objectives is not always due to intellect or special abilities.

We've all met folks who look to be successful but are less clever or have fewer credentials.

Along with other skills such as patience, ingenuity, and tenacity, the right attitude is often a key driver of success.

We all have a fundamental character that we can hide for a while but will eventually reveal.

If you have a pessimistic outlook on life, all endeavours to achieve your objectives would be futile.

When a key milestone is reached, it seems to inspire others to follow suit.

When Roger Bannister ran the mile in 3 minutes 59.4 seconds, it paved the way for many others to follow suit. Athletes' overall fitness has not altered much. When a person wins a world championship in a sport for a single year, it is because all parts of that person's game come together at the same moment and then magically vanish.

If you attend a social gathering when in a bad mood, you will have a terrible impression, although many others will have thought the same party was fantastic. Public speaking may be distressing for some people, but for others, depending on how they are affected by nervousness, the same individual might seem fairly calm.

When a person achieves success in a sport that requires certain talents, such as golf, they are sometimes told: "they are extremely fortunate."

Have you ever heard the expression, 'It's interesting how the more I practice, the luckier I become!'

Yes, practice will help you better. It will also boost your self-esteem.

The top players can picture a putt and do not anticipate missing it, whether it is 2 feet or 50 feet. It may be a little surprise when a putt misses, but the golfer is unconcerned and just plays the following stroke. They acquire confidence and perform better since they pre-visualize the task.

They are never concerned about failing. 'Get over it,' for example, might help you concentrate on the next step.

Self-belief

It's excellent to be confident in your abilities, as long as it doesn't border on arrogance. Maintain your confidence by convincing yourself that you will succeed and that you cannot fail. The idea is to 'not be concerned about failure.' Failure is a natural part of life; everyone fails. With the correct mindset, you will see good experiences from your mistakes as learning opportunities.

Modifying attitudes

While fundamental personalities will constantly reappear, you may adjust some of your preconceived notions and thoughts.

If you want to support a certain stream of thinking, repeat it to yourself throughout the day.

The term you pick should be one that you can readily see in a good light rather than a negative one.

'I want to develop my football abilities so I can keep the ball aloft 50 times,' for example. Instead of saying, 'I don't want to miss any more penalties this year,' use this.

The latter stresses failure rather than good performance improvement.

Instead of saying, 'I'm not going to watch any more television,' instead, 'I'll watch for an hour just at 6:00 p.m. as a special treat.'

If you are certain of your ambitions, you should tell others, particularly your family. But beware: individuals in the know may offer you bad comments if their attitude is negative, and they may indicate you will fail.

Chapter 5.2: Control Your Mindset

You've surely heard the tale of the professor who filled a jar with large rocks and then asked his students whether the jar seemed full. He then poured in gravel, sand, and water. The jar was never overflowing. That's because one of the most important rules of filling a jar—and of good time management—is to start with the biggest pebbles.

The following time management ideas, with little practice, will help you become more productive, creative—and successful.

1. Identify the big rocks first.

Look to identify the two or three most important chores that need to be accomplished every day. Set everything else aside until you've finished all, or almost all, of them. Finishing the most essential chores first in your day allows you to accomplish less important ones afterwards. Write out your top priorities for the week at the start of the week. Devote the first hour of each day to placing the large rocks (most important objectives) in the jar!

Prioritizing chores and managing your time effectively allow you to complete the most critical things on time.

2. Be mindful.

Distraction is the adversary of effective time management. Turn off your phone when you start working on your largest rocks. Close any unwanted browser windows. Take a long, deep breath. Set a timer for at least an hour of concentrated, conscious attention to your activity. If an hour is too lengthy, set a timer. Developing a mindfulness habit takes work, but it pays off handsomely.

3. Get in your zone.

You're not alone if your workday consists of a half-hour spent looking at a blank page and perusing the web. Many great professionals believe that finding the time and feeling motivated is the number one adversary of their creativity. (Creativity applies equally to engineers and salespeople as it does to authors and designers.) Remember that inspiration is more likely to arrive if you keep the door open and show up for any resultant brilliance. Setting time management tactics to block out time for creativity can help you get in the zone quicker, no matter how counterintuitive it seems. The more everyday routines you develop around developing attentive habits for completing your task, the more likely your outcomes will be effective.

4. Create habits.

The greatest method to create any Time Management habit is via repetition. If a certain activity causes your stomach to churn or your mind to wander, try to make it one of your greatest rocks for 90 days. Commit to completing the task without self-bargaining or distraction. Your most feared chore will most likely transform into something more doable over a week or two.

5. Organize weekly.

The more you simplify your procedures and reduce distractions, the simpler it will be to devote time to concentration, strategic thinking, and creativity. Take a few seconds to unsubscribe from any email lists that you no longer desire. Documents should be filed. Finish those two-minute activities and clean up your satellite desk. If you're hungry, eat something; and make that long-overdue appointment. By removing unneeded distractions (also known as time-sucks) from your daily routine, you will free up more brain space and boost concentration on important tasks.

6. Let freedom reign.

Even the most gifted individuals may get mired down in the minutia of day-to-day jobs and obligations. If you have a goal in mind (being promoted, finishing a brief, developing a killer app), you must account for both failures and achievements. This translates into scheduling time each day or week to "just do it." For an advertising writer, this may include brainstorming tagline ideas without regard for client regulations. For a software designer, this may mean allowing oneself to develop some poor code before getting it perfect. Knowing you have time to play makes it simpler to accomplish less creative activities.

7. Let it go.

For the parent readers, Disney's Frozen theme tune may get stuck in your mind. Apologies!

But there is a time for work and a time for leisure and relaxation. The aviation oxygen mask analogy is very appropriate here. Before you can genuinely flourish at work, you must first take care of yourself! Being as smart, productive, and engaged as a team member, manager, or leader is a crucial part of your continuous obligations. Nobody ever operates at full capacity all of the time. That is why taking time away from work is essential for job performance—it re-energizes you. So, when you say you're leaving the workplace, mean it. Your investment will provide a significant return.

Chapter 5.3: Fix Your Obsessions

Everyone nowadays is fascinated with productivity. Most individuals spend the majority of their lives telling themselves that they need to accomplish more to be happier, more successful, or richer. Many studies have demonstrated that being too productive may lead to decreased productivity and efficiency, while others suggest that workaholism is a widespread issue. There are things you may do to assist you to overcome your preoccupation with productivity.

Changing Your Mindset to Reduce Your Obsession

1. **Think positive thoughts.** Think good thoughts about your employment every day when you get home. Don't dwell on the bad, particularly what you didn't do. Instead, consider what you did do and how productive you were.

    - Consider the wonderful things you accomplished. Consider the job you completed, the individuals you assisted, and the stack of documents you completed.

    - Concentrate on how productive you were rather than how productive you believe you should have been.

2. **Shift your thought patterns about work.** Outside societal and cultural variables may contribute to people's addiction to work and productivity. It is certainly necessary to take pride in your profession and provide for yourself and your family, but you must equally recognize the value of your own non-work life. One method to do this is to change your perspective on work and personal life.

    - Start convincing yourself that your personal life is equally as vital as your job life to transform your perspective about work and personal life. For example, tell yourself, "My extracurricular activities are legitimate. They contribute to my achievement."

- Shifting your mindset requires you to pay equal attention to your non-work life as you do to your work life. This may be done in a variety of ways. You may strive to improve your connections with family and friends, expand yourself by finding new hobbies or pursuing interests, or set aside time for soothing and restorative activities.

3. **Avoid basing happiness on productivity.** When you put your happiness on your productivity, you miss out on chances to be joyful in the present. Setting goals is a good thing to do, but when your goal becomes an obsession and consumes all of your thoughts, you have a problem.

    - Ask yourself why you set the objectives that you did. Are these attainable objectives? Do you have unreasonable expectations for your goal's completion? If necessary, change your objective, create a new goal, or eliminate a goal.
    - Celebrate your accomplishments as you work toward a goal. This allows you to discover satisfaction while working or striving to reach a goal, rather than continually concentrating on the desire to do more.

4. **Refrain from basing self-worth on productivity.** You should no longer base your self-esteem on your degree of productivity. Just because you were more productive the day before or last year does not imply that you are a worse person. That doesn't imply you have to compensate by being extremely productive. Your self-esteem should be based on a variety of factors, not simply productivity.

5. **Focus on the present.** Obsession with productivity keeps you either in the past or in the future. Striving to be more productive keeps you focused on the future, but stressing about how you weren't productive keeps you focused on the past. Instead, concentrate on the present moment.

    - Get done what you can right now. Don't be concerned about yesterday or tomorrow. Work hard today, and when you're through, be proud of what you've achieved.
    - Don't berate yourself if you're unwell, tired, or not at your best. Instead of stressing about achieving less than you used to, concentrate on what you can do while being sick. Be pleased with the results.

Chapter 5.4: Avoid Distractions

My brain reminds me of Dug from the film "Up." When Dug, a dog, speaks, he is utterly sidetracked by the notion, sight, or sound of squirrels. This is what I call "squirrel brain."

The good thing about having a squirrel brain is that it allows me to easily produce fresh ideas and improvise a speech. The bad news about having a squirrel brain is that it makes it difficult for me to stay focused on a single topic or activity for an extended period.

What my squirrel brain wants to do is write a little bit of a blog post, then go work a little bit on a program I'm writing, then check Facebook to see what people in my group are saying, then check the weather forecast for tomorrow, then make some notes regarding my next client appointment.

This is counter-productive.

Any productivity guru will tell you that both distractions and attempting to multitask undermine our capacity to accomplish tasks.

Techniques for minimizing distractions and getting things done

I've built time-management approaches that connect brief bursts of concentrated effort since I know I'm a project sprinter, not a marathoner.

As a consequence, I can get a lot done and be very productive in ways that are doable for my squirrel-brained personality.

If you're like me and easily distracted, here's how you can increase your productivity:

1. Identify priorities

The first step is to ask yourself, "What are the most important chores that I need to do today?" Create a list or write them down. I like and utilize ToDoist.

2. Choose one thing to work on

Prioritize the top two or three items on your list. No, you are not permitted to choose more than that. Otherwise, you will get distracted. If you have a large job ahead of you, divide it into smaller tasks on your list. Then choose ONE ITEM. This is what you'll be working on next.

3. Set aside a chunk of time

You will now concentrate on the ONE THING you choose.

There is nothing else.

Many individuals use the Pomodoro Technique for productivity time. This technique recommends 25 minutes of work followed by a 5-minute rest.

I suggest selecting a time frame that works best for you. The key is your dedication. Choose a time frame of 20 minutes, 30 minutes, or an hour and commit to completing just one job.

4. Use a timer or an extension

A simple egg timer or a smartphone timing app would suffice. Simply place it near your keyboard or desk where it will be visible. Set it to run for the specified period. You may also use the Strict Workflow Chrome plugin, which I use.

Strict Workflow is fantastic since you can configure it to close any site that is distracting you. My social networking platforms include Facebook, Twitter, LinkedIn, and Reddit. I've also added a slew of news websites since I'm easily caught up in the political drama.

5. Use a notepad or sticky note

Write down the one job you need to do on a single sheet of paper. Place it on your pc.

Look at it often.

This is your mission; remember it, perform it, and finish it. Ask yourself, "Am I now on task?" Or am I becoming disoriented?

You will be given brief breaks at whatever period you have selected whether you are utilizing Strict Workflow, the Pomodoro approach, or any variant. If you haven't finished your one job before the end of your break, you'll work on it during your next sprint.

6. Eliminate distractions

Turn off your computer, email, and phone – or step away from them.

Self-Control (Mac) and Cold Turkey (PC) are two more programs you may use to prevent yourself from social media and other sites where you spend time. Cold Turkey appeals to me since it allows you to set aside time for the whole week.

Making a practice of disconnecting for a certain period each day may help you achieve your main objectives.

7. Spend time with the squirrels

Our squirrels need affection. They get irritated if they do not receive care.

Set your timer for five minutes at the end of your time block and spend it with the squirrels. Do you need to check your email or send a text?

Need to stretch or read the New York Times? Do you want to check your Facebook or Twitter?

You can do it right now - in five minutes.

And it's OK if you utilize social media for company promotion. However, that should be its race. Make sure you utilize the opportunity to sell your company rather than being drawn down a rabbit hole of chitter-chatter. The Facebook news feed eradicator is another plugin I use on my PC (where I work).

This allows me to write posts and join groups without being drawn into talks about the unusual weather that a buddy has begun. I do it from my phone in the evening.

8. Rinse and repeat

It's time to move on after you've completed your one task.

Choose the next priority from the list you prepared at the start of the day.

Continue to step two by selecting the next task or work component. Then go through the list many times more.

Following this time management approach has helped me.

Give it a go and see if it makes you more productive.

Chapter 5.5: Set Daily Goals

What are daily goals?

Our daily goals are objectives that we want to reach by the end of the day. A goal is something toward which we concentrate our efforts. Daily objectives might be as grandiose as you want.

They are most likely part of your broader, long-term objectives, or they may be something you wish to perform every day, such as developing excellent habits.

When we think about goal setting, we may only think of large objectives that take a long time to fulfil and need a lot of work. But don't be fooled: everyday objectives need hard work and effort.

Why is setting daily goals important?

Some of our objectives will take a long time to complete, which is acceptable. It's a positive thing. Patience is essential. Daily objectives, on the other hand, are essential for keeping us grounded in the present. They compel us to consider our circumstances presently, not tomorrow or next week.

We are more productive when we create daily objectives. We're always making action plans, and they teach us the value of planning. Our daily objectives also make us feel productive, which helps us remain motivated.

Samantha Kris, an author and public speaker, delivered a TedTalk about making goals that matter, explaining that we need to make objectives that line with our values and benefit us and how we want our futures to be.

We cannot follow others' goal-setting routes; instead, we must construct one for ourselves.

Kris' assertion is correct. Prioritizing our objectives, no matter how large or little, helps us strive toward living a meaningful life that we can be proud of. We may learn how to make daily objectives at work that will benefit us professionally or personally. Our higher aspirations become more manageable as a result.

4 tips for setting daily goals

Just because you want to learn how to establish objectives every day doesn't imply it will happen overnight. Knowing what objectives work best for you requires effort and self-awareness.

Before you begin writing your first set of daily objectives and working to attain them, consider the following four suggestions:

1. Make sure your goals are SMART

Goals may be set without much thinking, but SMART goals are the polar opposite. They guarantee that you create defined, attainable, and time-bound objectives.

Your action plan is well-thought-out, with specifics that point you on the right path. Goals may be SMART even if they are simple and integrated into your routine.

2. Don't set too many goals

It's OK to be enthusiastic about goal planning, but don't overdo it. This is also a good time to clarify the distinction between objectives and tasks.

Daily objectives should be linked to monthly and long-term objectives. Otherwise, it's simply a job. That isn't to say it isn't required – picking up the dog from the vet is important — but it isn't likely to advance any aims. You must also be realistic about how much you can do in a single day.

In your daily routine, consider your time frame and how long each aim will take (and around those critical tasks). Remember that you don't have to complete ten tasks every day.

You may focus on some of these tomorrow or make them monthly objectives. This will also help you celebrate your key accomplishments when they come.

3. Practice writing down your goals

Let's face it, we all forget stuff now and again. When we make our daily objectives, we should write them down so that we don't forget and can concentrate more on them.

One research conducted by psychology professor Dr Gail Matthews at Dominican University in California discovered that persons who wrote down their objectives were more likely to attain them.

Participants were more responsible and dedicated to the objectives they had set for themselves.

4. Check to see whether your objectives align with your beliefs.

Consider your values for a minute. What kinds of objectives are compatible with them? The daily objectives we establish should reflect our desired lifestyle and what is essential to us. Smaller actions that coincide with your principles help you achieve both professional and personal objectives.

They may grow into broader ambitions that expose us to new chances and experiences. When setting your objectives, keep in mind your ultimate aims with your activities.

When is the best time to write daily goals?

This section may create some disagreement. We must understand when to create daily objectives to fulfil them. What is most important is that you set them.

Writing down your objectives in the morning establishes your intentions for the day. They'll help you get started and concentrate for the remainder of the day, as well as keep them fresh in your memory.

If you prefer to establish your daily objectives first thing in the morning, make sure you allow adequate time in your morning routine. The last thing you want is to feel hurried and pressed while outlining your critical duties.

However, this might be a method of focusing oneself and finding some peace in an otherwise hectic morning.

Setting objectives in the evening of the previous night is a whole different experience. It enables you to brainstorm for the next day after thinking about the previous day. Perhaps you did not complete a task that you desired, or a brilliant idea occurred to you.

Writing down your objectives the night before or at the end of the day might assist you in planning ahead of time. If you know your morning will be busy, writing them in the evening eliminates one item from your to-do list.

Perhaps you have no notion of what works best for you. Finding out is the greatest method to tackle this. Change it up the next time you sit down to set your daily objectives.

Chapter 6: All about Productivity

Chapter 6.1: Productivity and Productivity Levels

Politicians, economists, and commentators discuss it on a broad scale. Business owners and managers are concerned about their teams and workers that operate in a hybrid environment. And most of us make some judgment about the

there we "feel" productive on any particular day.

Is that what you mean?

Not exactly. Productivity may imply various things in different circumstances, particularly as knowledge work and automation become more prevalent. Understanding the many levels of productivity may help you comprehend how your productivity at work contributes to the productivity of your firm, and how both connect to the productivity of your nation.

Productivity evaluates how successfully a country converts labour and materials (the input) into commodities and services (the output, GDP). It is a comprehensive indicator that reflects policy and technological advancements and demonstrates economic health concerning other factors in the macro-environment. It's not very useful for considering your productivity.

Productivity assesses how successful firms create money from inputs such as labour and materials. Business productivity is often defined as revenue divided by hours worked. An aggregate productivity level is unlikely to give practical insights to corporate executives, but it may assist them to assess how they compare to competitors or other top organizations.

Productivity at the firm level – revenue compared to employee work hours in a quarter — might seem distant from our efforts, which may yield results or give value on a different timescale.

People conceive of "being productive" in terms of what they individually accomplish. For many individuals, this entails crossing items off their "to-do" list. This level of personal productivity indicates your efficiency in accomplishing activities. But not all chores are created equal, and does it matter whether they are completed effectively or just completed?

Unfortunately, measuring personal productivity at work or in life may be difficult, particularly now that many individuals don't undertake repetitive jobs - it used to be much simpler to assess productivity by how many widgets a person made every hour.

Personal productivity is a contentious issue in the era of knowledge labour. Creativity and innovation, as well as exceptional customer service, do not neatly add up to a gauge of efficiency. Nonetheless, consider what productivity implies in your job and sort of work:

- What is the best technique to evaluate quality or value?
- What is the relevant measure of quantity?
- What are the inputs we want to use most efficiently?

Then, whatever the statistic, strive to create the circumstances for improvement:

The most important output to consider for your teams and yourself is value. Productivity = (work value) / (employee time, effort).

The value may be difficult to establish, but you may begin by considering the results. Something is important to you (or to a corporation) when it assists you in achieving your goals. Not every job on your to-do list is equal in terms of the value it provides to you or others.

This shifts our perspective on productivity to include how well an activity generates value as well as how efficiently we do that activity. The value of work in a firm is determined by how well it corresponds with the organization's goals, the quality with which it is performed, and the speed with which it is completed.

Productivity Levels

Becoming effective with your time is one of the pillars of being an exceptional workplace leader. Most individuals are tremendously busy, but the issue is always whether you are busy being busy or busy accomplishing what is essential.

The six degrees of productivity that I think individuals experience at work are listed below.

Which level do you spend the most of your time on?

Level 1: Avoiding — People purposefully avoid doing their tasks. That is a lot of procrastination.

Level 2: Distracted — They are easily sidetracked by incoming priorities other than the ones they are meant to be concentrating on. They are overwhelmed by their workload. As a result, people must work three times as hard to complete one unit of labour.

Level 3: Appropriate — This is where they are performing the job that they "should" be doing, or just doing what is necessary.

Level 4: Deliberate — People are becoming more diligent in their job at this point. They have a methodical approach to managing their Quarter, week, and day.

Level 5: Important — This is where employees do important work that is essential to their unique function. They consistently work on a core category or the main project in a methodical manner. Things begin to shift at this point. One unit of input generates 10 units of output.

Level 6: Inspired Work — Work that is inspired is game-changing work. This is where you will generate ideas or discover activities that will make a difference. You can accomplish one unit of labour and get up to fifty units of output while doing game-changing work. Tim Ferriss refers to this as "Leveraged Activities." The actions that have a high effect.

Chapter 6.2: Professional Productivity

Ask any small- to medium-sized company owner for advice on how to be more productive. They probably wear a lot of hats — CEO, business development person, marketing person, human resources person, IT guy, and so forth — and have mastered a few tricks to simplify their operations and make the most of their days. Here are some of the most productive professionals' top behaviours.

They prioritize and protect their time.

Highly productive individuals understand where their energy is best spent and can concentrate their time and attention accordingly. That is, they understand how to say no, create and maintain boundaries, and delegate duties to others. Are you still working on it? The good news is that skills like prioritizing and establishing limits are essential for success — and they can be practised and taught.

Highly productive individuals have learnt to successfully split their time between urgent and vital duties like deadline-driven projects and crisis response and non-urgent but significant chores like relationship-building, personal growth, and health care. They minimize time spent on "busy work" or low-value things such as endlessly scanning the web.

They make the most of their time.

Highly productive individuals not only aggressively concentrate and focus their time, but they also optimize little pockets of time that others would squander. They could, for example, listen to podcasts on their commute or spend the 10 minutes between meetings replying to the email.

They're well organized.

Highly productive individuals do not waste time and attention searching for a phone number or a missing file. They have processes in place to locate what they need when they want it. Mobile applications specialized in your sector may assist you in staying on top of a variety of issues. Applications may help you monitor billable hours on the move if you're an attorney, or if you supervise service employees in the field, job dispatching apps can help you prevent overbooking your team or showing up late for an appointment. Other popular productivity tools for small company owners include Evernote, a note-taking software, and LinkedIn Pulse, which keeps you up to date on industry news.

They avoid procrastination and distractions.

Of course, if you're not cautious, applications, email, and other technology may become distractions rather than productivity helps. According to Hillary Rettig, productivity coach and author of The Seven Secrets of the Prolific: The Definitive Guide to Overcoming Procrastination, Perfectionism, and Writer's Block, "productive professionals realize that occasionally they need to withdraw and concentrate on the work at hand." This may be accomplished by either unplugging your computer from the Internet while working or turning off notifications and the ringtone on your phone. Make it simple for yourself, says Rettig, who adds that "productive individuals never spend time trying to 'raise their willpower': they merely identify and overcome productivity hurdles."

They invest in the right tools.

While it may seem reasonable and wise to postpone investing in better technology, another app, a new website, or other things or services until your firm is more successful, this strategy may harm you. Productive individuals invest in the necessary resources and tools to help their companies grow. If businesses still use paper forms for things like invoicing, purchase orders, and staff scheduling, for example, you may save time and money by switching to mobile forms and a secure cloud-based storage solution.

They automate everything possible.

Why waste time on jobs that aren't necessary? Paying bills, collecting money from consumers, sorting and replying to emails, making social media updates, and other time-consuming operations may now be automated thanks to advances in technology. Make a list of the tasks you perform on a daily or weekly basis and see if any of them may be automated. Hootsuite, for example, may assist you in automating your social media activities. (Just remember to adhere to the do's and don'ts!)

Chapter 6.3: Long-Term Productivity

Align Goals With Your Interests

Let's start with long-term objectives since they are the ones that define your life and influence your activities over time. A choice to attend university, for example, will shape the framework of many years of your life but will affect your whole adulthood.

The first significant insight concerning long-term planning concerns perception. People often overestimate how much can be completed in six months or even a year, while underestimating how much can be accomplished in three, five, or ten years. The reason for this is that individuals are frequently overconfident in their talents, without taking into account their restrictions (i.e., unexpected occurrences, side-tasks, etc.), yet they do not function effectively on a larger scale of events. This makes sense when you consider someone in their 30s - five years is one-sixth of their whole life!

As a consequence of this skewed viewpoint, long-term objectives should be planned over a long timescale and SHOULD be ambitious — for example, trying to finish a marathon in six months may be incredibly ambitious for some, while preparing to complete an ultramarathon in four years may be completely doable. This seems to be a contradiction, but we'll explain why it works later.

The second critical insight is that our long-term objectives should be as closely connected with our philosophy, values, and personality as feasible. This is not always achievable, particularly in job-related areas (unless you work for a firm that you like, as we do at CodeLathe), but the better you feel about what you do, the more likely you are to achieve your objectives.

This remark is equally essential while making objectives. If you despise running but want to include some movement into your life, choose the alternative but related objectives, such as cycling or swimming. The objective here is to think about what you love and what is important to you before setting goals based on those principles.

Another example: maybe you want to make a lot of money and you like vehicles. An abstract aim of earning millions of dollars per year may not be enough incentive, but imagining a collection of luxury automobiles may. That is the purpose of this exercise; we want to end up with 20-30 long-term objectives divided into areas such as health, job, social life, personal development, and so on. These may vary over time; these objectives are intended to be readily evaluated and altered in the coming years.

Be SMART

I said that the list should include 20-30 aggressive objectives. How can we tell whether their objectives are good or bad? This is a rather basic task. A good aim is SMART. Let's go through the concept:

- **Specific** – The objective is clear and provides no room for interpretation.
- **Measurable** – Progress toward the objective should be measurable.
- **Achievable** – The aim should be achievable (even if it is grandiose!)
- **Relevant** – It should be meaningful to the individual.
- **Time-bound** – The completion timetable should be specified.

Let's take a quick look at why a single objective must be SMART. We'll also go through other cases that aren't SMART and may be more difficult to complete.

It will be difficult to organize the following actions if a goal is not detailed enough. The phrase "I want to start a business" doesn't reveal anything about the real ambition. In other nations, forming a corporation takes just a few hours. This is also strongly tied to measurability; a goal that simply states, "I want to travel more," is not verifiable; we must explain what "more" implies. "I want to spend two months a year abroad for three years straight," for example, with specific and verifiable goals.

As I previously said, our objectives should be high so that there is always something driving us ahead. On the other hand, the objective must be attainable; otherwise, it will instil feelings of failure and defeatism, both of which are significant demotivators toward any goal.

As an example, consider running. Is it a stretch to complete the Ultra Trail Mount Blanc (UTMB) run? Yes, it is. Is it feasible? Of course, hundreds of runners participate in this race each year. A plan to conduct a Mars landing in the next three years, on the other hand, is not feasible given our existing knowledge and technological capabilities. The same can be said about swimming underwater for 45 minutes without diving equipment - certain things are just beyond our technical and physical ability, and we should set our objectives appropriately.

We discussed relevancy in the last part; once you've decided on a goal, it's much simpler to pursue it since you have that internal driving component.

Setting time limitations on when the objective should be completed is another critical factor. Unless the deadline is approaching, it is human nature to delay and postpone activities. It is simpler to design smaller actions that contribute to your ultimate objective within shorter periods when you have a well-defined limit.

Divide and Conquer

We must begin working toward completion after our long-term objectives have been determined. This is a vital element in any planning process: what should be our next course of action? Time is finite, and productivity is primarily about navigating between those constraints.

As stated in the preceding paragraph, goals should be ambitious (remember, they are long-term objectives). The issue is that they may seem unattainable at first. For this part, we'll use the UTMB run as an example. This is a 170km run with an elevation gain of 10,000m. When you think about it, it seems impossible, doesn't it?

The trick is to break down that "impossible" long-term objective into smaller, more manageable parts. Setting a handful of intermediate sub-goals is the best method to do this. Assume you can run 10 kilometres without any effort. A half-marathon would be an excellent beginning step. This may be a reasonable six-month goal. The following year, the next stage may be to run a marathon. Another objective is to do a sky marathon in two years, and the last target before the primary goal is to finish a shorter ultra-marathon in four years. With this description of objectives, you might finish the UTMB in 6-7 years.

This objective suddenly becomes attainable with time and a lot of motivation, which is the most critical aspect. You begin by training for a half-marathon, then a marathon, and so on. In the end, you may not even complete the primary objective, but the actions you do along the way will help you significantly - you will develop a healthy habit of running consistently, and you will most likely modify your lifestyle to make time for extended activities.

So, how should those intermediate phases be defined? This is a difficult issue with no hard and fast rules. It is dependent on each activity, which is why each objective must be quantifiable.

Once we've identified a few intermediate phases, we should begin preparing around them in a more timely manner. In our case, we intended to finish the half-marathon in six months. That would imply three to four runs each week on average, each consuming 30-90 minutes of your time. You pick a solid training regimen, add it to your calendar, and you're set. If you, do it for all 20-30 long-term objectives, you'll be incredibly busy, but productive! All of your activities will lead you to achieve significant objectives that will enhance your life. And what a lovely sensation!

Execute

You must be accountable for carrying out any shorter-term plans after they have been recognized and prepared. This is the most difficult stage since we are always presented with new responsibilities and challenges. Take these into consideration and don't schedule your days from 6 a.m. to 11 p.m. Making time in your calendar to react to unforeseen occurrences can make your journey less rough and simpler to navigate.

Another excellent strategy to improve in many areas is to develop habits. This is an essential issue that will be addressed in the series' following instalment.

Chapter 6.4: Productivity in Economics

Increases in labour productivity, which simply implies how effectively we do things, drive long-term economic development. In other words, how well does a country employ its labour and other resources? Labour productivity is the number of products produced by each employee per unit of time worked. To appreciate labour productivity, consider a Canadian worker who can produce 10 loaves of bread in an hour against a US worker who can only create two loaves of bread in the same hour. Canadians are more productive in this fictitious case. Being more productive fundamentally implies being able to do more in the same amount of time. This frees up resources that may be utilized elsewhere.

What factors influence worker productivity? The solution is self-evident. Physical capital, human capital, and technological development are the primary factors of worker productivity. These are also important components of economic development.

Physical capital may be conceived of as the tools that employees use. Physical capital, more officially, comprises not only the plant and equipment utilized by businesses but also infrastructures, such as roads and other components of transportation networks that contribute to the economy. Governments provide infrastructure. Again, more physical capital means increased production. Physical capital may improve productivity in two ways: (1) an increase in physical capital quantity (for example, more computers of the same quality); and (2) an increase in physical capital quality the (same number of computers but the computers are faster, and so on). Human capital is the cumulative knowledge (through school and experience), skills, and competence of an economy's typical worker. The higher an economy's average degree of education, the greater its cumulative human capital labour productivity. Human capital and physical capital accumulation are comparable in that investment today pay in future longer-term production.

Technology is another aspect that influences worker productivity.

Technological change is a mix of invention (advances in knowledge) and innovation (the application of that advance in a new product or service). The transistor, for example, was created in 1947. It enabled us to reduce the size of electrical equipment and consume less power than previous tube technologies. Since then, advances in technology have resulted in smaller and better transistors, which are now found in items as diverse as smartphones, computers, and escalators. The invention of the transistor enabled people to work from anywhere using smaller gadgets. These gadgets may be used to interact with coworkers, measure product quality, or do any other activity in less time, hence increasing worker productivity.

Most people associate new technology with the introduction of new items such as the laser, the smartphone, or some new wonder medication. Another example of technology in food production is the creation of more drought-resistant seeds. However, technology, as economists define it, encompasses much more. It includes novel means of arranging labour, such as the creation of the assembly line, new techniques for assuring higher output quality in factories, and innovative organizations that help with the process of transforming inputs into output. In summary, technology includes any advancements that enable current machines and other inputs to create more and at greater quality, as well as whole new items.

Chapter 6.5: Product Management

One of the most crucial skills a product manager should have is time management. It enables the product manager to establish appropriate priorities. There are frequently so many things to accomplish while working on a project that only time management skills and strategy can assist.

As a result, a successful product manager should be able to manage their time effectively. Surprisingly, they can benefit from some time management advice. So, in this piece, we will provide the top four time-management ideas for product managers to help them steer and produce better results.

Time Management Tips for Product Managers

Strategic Planning and Mapping

Before beginning work on the product, the product manager should plan the product's development, launch, and marketing. The estimated delivery time and marketing should be included in the planning; this will assist the product manager to establish his priorities correctly.

Furthermore, the budget and team members should be taken into account. The product manager should ensure that each team member adheres to their responsibilities and delivers on schedule. The product's launching date must also be considered.

Delegation

This is also a useful time-saving tip. A good product manager should be able to assign responsibilities and functions. There are times when there are so many things to accomplish that nothing gets done until tasks are distributed or shared. For best delivery, duties or tasks should be shared or assigned to the appropriate team members. This saves a lot of time and keeps team members from becoming exhausted.

Avoiding Social Media and Other Distractions

Social media usage may be addicting, particularly for those who are tech-savvy. A product manager working on a deadline should avoid wasting time on social media and other distractions. Every day, they should plan their duties and follow through on them. All forms of distractions should be avoided.

Multi-tasking

This is a crucial time-saving ability. As a product manager, you should multitask, and you should encourage the rest of the team to do the same. This implies that you and the other members of the team should be able to accomplish several things and carry out multiple activities at the same time.

Have Shorter Meetings

If you've worked in product management, you've probably been forced to sit through more than one meeting that you wanted would conclude as quickly as possible. Most meetings are way too lengthy, and some are not even necessary. Meetings have the potential to hinder productivity, so reducing them in half or eliminating some of them is a step in the right direction for effective time management.

Chapter 6.6: Workplace Productivity

Workplace productivity is the efficiency with which activities and objectives for the firm are performed. Profitability and employee morale will be more visible as a result of building a productive workplace.

Having a productive staff is an area of business that many businesses struggle with. Finding the most effective techniques to boost productivity and emphasizing the benefits of maximum productivity will result in a better general knowledge of what workplace productivity is.

Given that workplace productivity is essentially accomplishing tasks on time, it is critical to understand how to do so without losing job quality. This implies that staff must be right in addition to being speedy. If maximum production is the goal, efficiency cannot be overlooked.

Employees may perform a variety of things to improve efficiency and, ultimately, workplace productivity. Getting rid of distractions is one of the first steps in achieving efficiency and productivity in today's technology age. This often entails shutting off personal mobile phones, banning social media on work computers, and even switching off music with lyrics.

It is also advised to prioritize the least favoured task on your to-do list first thing in the morning. While tackling the easier duties first may seem to be a good way to ease into the workday, you are putting off the tasks that take more effort. You will most likely run out of steam before the end of the day and will have to postpone those activities until the following day.

However, some individuals are less productive in the mornings. It is critical to determine your personal most productive hours. Once those hours are determined, scheduling jobs based on difficulty inside those periods will aid in achieving the best degree of efficiency.

The most efficient day will not only be planned but will also be followed. A daily to-do list and a timer will help you to guarantee that no time is wasted and that the necessary chores are completed at the most efficient times. If a task takes longer than expected, assess the problem and figure out how to better.

Goal setting has a significant impact on efficiency. While a to-do list might serve as a form of daily objective, other goals, such as sales this week or total words written today, can provide significant positive results. Whatever it is that your firm wishes to achieve in the long run should be put down and seriously pursued.

Although some employees believe that taking a break is a waste of time, it may assist to clear the mind and allow for more productive working hours. When the brain spends so much time on a single job without a break, it might be difficult to generate fresh knowledge or ideas on the subject. This is why taking 10-15 minute breaks throughout the day might boost productivity.

When your work area is clean and well-organized, productivity increases. Making certain that goods are where they should be not only save time spent searching for them, but it may also aid in the thinking process. We may easily lose our line of thought when we have to pause during our most productive hours to seek a document. Getting back into the appropriate frame of mind after looking for that paper may be difficult, and therefore a productivity killer.

Surprisingly, multitasking does not increase productivity or efficiency. In reality, juggling many projects at once would most certainly reduce the quality of the work and make it take longer in the long run. While it may seem that so much is being completed, avoiding multitasking and doing activities one at a time can save both quality and time.

A corporation and its workers will realize that productivity delivers several rewards by taking the time to learn how to be more efficient. Concentrating on the positives will assist to motivate change.

CHAPTER 7: MAXIMIZE YOUR WORK PRODUCTIVITY

Chapter 7.1: Learn Smart Strategies

We all have the same amount of time in a day, and there is no way to make it longer. It makes no difference how powerful or affluent one is; we are all limited to 24 hours every day.

We must deduct time for sleeping, eating, commuting, and just living our daily lives; the time left for entrepreneurial chores is seldom sufficient. But there is a technique to make the most of that time, and it entails working smarter rather than harder. If you follow the eight ideas below, you will be able to do more in less time.

1. Make certain that you like what you do.

This is rather straightforward. When you like what you do, it does not seem to be labour. It sounds so corny, yet it's spot on. I like what I do and look forward to the day ahead every morning. It doesn't matter whether I had a late night or a long travel day; I get out of bed without an alarm clock every morning.

When you are genuinely enthusiastic about what you do, you maintain laser-like concentration, which naturally leads to great productivity. If you are unhappy and dislike what you do, regardless of how much money you make, you will not be enthusiastic, and your productivity will suffer.

2. Embrace technology.

You will be at a significant disadvantage if you fail to accept technology. There are browser extensions, applications, and automation tools available to assist with almost every area of your company and day-to-day duties.

Years ago, it became conceivable to operate your complete company from your laptop while on the road. Today, you can do the same thing with your mobile device. We have fantastic technologies at our disposal that allow us total geographic independence. Work on work while travelling, performing cardio at the gym, or waiting for a trip – having your whole business at your fingertips may boost your productivity significantly.

3. Leverage your networking relationships.

Consider how much time and effort you put into networking, such as being active on social media, attending conferences, and chatting with everyone. Take the time to build a strong network and use the power of others to support your company.

You must first give before you can expect to get, therefore make an effort to assist as many people as possible. The connections you form while doing this will come in helpful later on, and when you have a network of professionals to assist you in certain areas, you not only learn from the best, but you also don't have to do all of the heavy lifting alone.

4. Measure success in tasks completed, not hours worked.

Many individuals are preoccupied with the number of hours they work. Instead of stating, "I worked 12 hours today," emphasize the number of things you performed. Hours worked are meaningless when you are an entrepreneur since you are not punching a clock. Success is determined by the number of tasks done rather than the number of hours worked.

You get more done when you learn to complete jobs faster. Most entrepreneurs are inherently competitive, so set up a personal competition and attempt to improve your daily job completion rate. If you do this, your productivity will skyrocket.

5. Delegate your weaknesses.

I was continuously exhausted until I learnt to delegate. We sometimes believe we are superhuman and can achieve anything, but this is not the reality. No entrepreneur is perfect at everything, so identify your flaws and outsource those jobs to team members who are better qualified to manage them.

Rather than attempting to juggle a million jobs, concentrate on the ones you excel at and delegate the rest. This alone has the potential to transform your company. Never be hesitant to call ie professionals; the sooner you accept that you cannot handle everything, the more productive you will become.

6. Focus on consistent progress.

You won't be able to cross the finish line in a single day. The beginning of every business journey is often unpleasant, but as you develop, you learn how to deal with it and begin to chip away at your objectives. The key to success is consistency.

You will ultimately reach your goal if you concentrate on making progress every day and continue moving ahead. When you are preoccupied with making progress, you will learn how to perform activities more effectively while remaining focused on what is important.

7. Eliminate all distractions.

Distractions come in a variety of kinds and sizes, and the sooner you eliminate them from your life, the quicker you will be able to get back on track. Keeping such distractions out of your life assists you to stay focused.

You almost have to be a bit selfish and prioritize your aspirations and well-being above the sentiments of others. There are family, friends, and connections that may improve your performance; embrace them and keep them near.

8. Avoid procrastination by creating micro-goals.

Procrastination stifles productivity, and one of the most prevalent reasons for procrastination is a sense of failure. We all have big objectives, and if you attempt to attain them without breaking them down into smaller ones, you'll feel overwhelmed.

Divide your objectives into micro-goals. This enables you to finish things and feel successful. When there is little progress, the biggest ambitions seem to be within grasp.

Chapter 7.2: Minimum Input Maximum Output

Isn't a drastic life change too much like hard work? Here's how to achieve the best outcomes with the least amount of work.

Drink Water

Oh *yawn* "Blah, blah drink water…" you've heard this all before, right?

But do you understand why you should drink water?

Our bodies are composed of around 60% water and over 37 trillion cells, all of which are continually replenishing.

Technically, the body you have today isn't the one you were born with since, over time, every cell has utilized the water you've consumed and replaced itself.

Woah.

Your body will not be able to regenerate itself as effectively if you do not drink anything.

The NHS advises drinking eight to ten large glasses of water every day.

That's so refreshing.

Take 10,000 daily steps

To lose weight, you don't have to join a gym or go on a strict diet.

You just must ensure that you burn more calories than you consume, and 10,000 steps a day is a decent guideline to follow.

Walking around your home, walking the stairs, or getting off the bus one stop early will all add up, and all you need is a pedometer and some comfy shoes to track your progress.

Ten minutes meditation

Practising quieting your thoughts for a few minutes each day is said to make individuals happier, healthier, more creative, and less anxious.

According to certain studies, frequent meditators had a 48% lower risk of having a heart attack.

Try installing a meditation app like headspace.com (over a million downloads) and zoning out for 10 minutes.

Sit up Straight

Aside from making you seem like a disgruntled adolescent, poor posture may have a severe impact on your mental health.

Erik Peper, a behavioural scientist, conducted an experiment that demonstrated that when a person sits up straight, they are more likely to think of something positive or have a positive memory, as opposed to when a person walks slowly with a slumped posture, which causes them to feel tired and lacklustre.

We already know that we should eat at least five pieces of fruit and vegetables every day, much like the whole drinking water thing.

But how are we going to have fresh veggies in our fridge if we only go to the grocery once a week?

We've probably got a few bendy carrots, a sad bag of lettuce that "still looks OK," and a tin of sweetcorn.

However, you can purchase a wide range of frozen veggies and fruit at the store that is just as healthy as fresh fruit and vegetables but is frozen in time until you're ready to eat them.

Stock up on greens in the freezer and you'll never run out.

Lentils Lentils Lentils!

Are you tired of eating potatoes every night? Tired of the same old bread in your lunchbox? Then look no further, since wonderful lentils may be the solution to your healthy supper issues.

Lentils are flavorful, low in calories, and low in fat, yet they nevertheless leave you feeling full and pleased.

They have also been shown to help decrease cholesterol and maintain your heart in good working order.

They're high in fibre (for digestion) and protein (for cells), and the best part is that stores offer packets of prepared lentils that are already cooked in several delightful ways, so all you have to do is open the bag.

Breaking the habit

Every evening, many of us unknowingly exceed the prescribed alcohol limit by reaching for the wine.

We're only meant to have one glass of wine or one pint of beer each day, which, practically, isn't occurring in many homes.

However, you may attempt to stop the habit by diverting yourself with something else, such as tossing the contents of your briefcase down the stairs if you're constantly tempted to take a glass of wine around 6 pm.

It will take you an hour to gather everything, and by 7 p.m., the desire to consume wine may have gone.

Please let us know if this works...

If the shoe doesn't fit...

Ladies (and gentlemen) will all have experienced the agonizing sensation of wearing shoes that pinch, rub, create blisters, and overall make you want to scream at them.

Furthermore, 65% of leisure sports enthusiasts are wearing inappropriate footwear for the activity they are participating in.

Forget about appearance; what counts most is foot comfort and support.

Do you want to be 99 years old and walking about on smashed-up feet that are twisted like two paper clips?

No. No, you don't.

Wake up fresh

It is suggested that you get at least five hours of sleep every night.

Anything less, and things will become weird (moodiness, falling, hallucinations ("Did I see Elvis at the Co-op?" etc.).

Sleep with the curtains open to assist yourself in waking up in the morning.

When the sun rises and your brain detects light, it will begin to assist you in beginning to wake up before your alarm goes off.

Invest in a lightbox to replicate early sunshine instead for the dreary winter mornings.

Chapter 7.3: How to Improve Work Efficiency to Increase Productivity

Have you ever felt that you're not accomplishing enough at work? Every morning, you arrive at work with a specific plan and objectives for the day. However, there are moments when you feel as though you have not accomplished enough. This is not due to a lack of competence on your part. It is the things you are doing incorrectly and neglecting to incorporate into your professional routine. Workplace productivity is a critical problem from both an organizational and personal standpoint. So, how can you increase your productivity and efficiency? Let us investigate.

Why is it vital to increase your workplace productivity?

The obvious response to this topic is to improve organizational competency. You are not the only employee in your place of employment. You are a member of a team that is counting on you to fulfil your job. Everyone in the organization works together to make the organization better. There will be several consequences if you are not productive. You will not only reduce your drive, but you will also stifle organizational progress.

Increasing production helps to improve staff morale. They will be driven to achieve better, resulting in higher organizational production.

Customer satisfaction will rise as a result of enhanced performance and productivity. According to research, more efficient businesses retain more customers. Being productive is also crucial in terms of customer service.

However, the employee is not solely responsible for being productive. The business must instil in its personnel a productive and growing mentality. The organization's strategic objectives and vision should encompass the personal development of its personnel. The general idea is that if you take care of your people, your company will take care of them.

10 Ways to Increase Work Efficiency

Improving workplace productivity and efficiency is critical. But the issue is, how are you going to accomplish it? Here are a few ideas to get you started.

Avoid multitasking

Getting a lot of tasks done at once may seem to be efficient. That, however, is the polar opposite of being productive. When you multitask, you effectively divide your attention and effort. As a consequence, the end product may not be as excellent as it may have been if you had worked on it alone. It also ends up taking longer. As a result, it's best to avoid multitasking.

Set realistic goals

You won't be able to do a week's worth of work in a single day. The human intellect is not without restrictions. If you set an unreasonable target for yourself, you will wind up working longer hours, but your productivity will suffer as a result. You will experience energy burnout, lowering your overall level of efficiency.

Taking break

Don't overwork yourself like a machine. The brain needs a pause at its optimal level as well. The more you force it to work, the more it will slouch. It is advised that you take breaks at regular times throughout the day. This will refresh your mind and allow you to focus more effectively.

Stop finding perfection

It is a frequent fallacy that you must perform something again and over until perfection is reached. In truth, ultimate perfection can never be found. There is always the possibility that things may improve. As a result, you should not be bogged down by a single issue. Give it your all and go on to the next one.

Minimize interruptions

The idea is to work smarter, not harder. You should reconsider where you spend your time and how you spend your time. Rather than packing your calendar with more and more work, consider ways to limit interruptions to your job. Take initiatives where you can work for a long amount of time without being distracted, whether it is restricting your engagement with your coworkers or turning off your phone's notifications.

The two-minute rule

This is a general norm that everyone should adhere to. The two-minute rule asserts that if a task can be performed in two minutes or less, it should be completed immediately and without interruption. Instead of creating large goals for yourself, break them down into smaller targets or micro-goals. It will be easy to check off those feasible goals if they are placed in short time frames.

Set your deadline

Procrastination has a much greater impact on productivity than you would think. When you pile things up till the last minute, it just adds up. This will cause you to multitask or hurry your job, lowering the quality. Instead of adhering to the organizational deadline, set your own. Try to keep to it so you don't fall behind the time.

Reduce meetings

This may seem counterintuitive at first. However, you should aim to avoid needless meetings. Most official responsibilities may be efficiently assigned through memos or email in this day and age of linked communication. Attending meaningless meetings is just a waste of your time and productivity.

Wake up early

CEOs that are successful get up as early as 4 a.m. This is merely a statistic to demonstrate that waking up early gives you more time to get things done. If you can, go for a run or a stroll. This will not only clear your thoughts but will also get you ready for the day.

Learn to say 'no'

Now and again, you will see your supervisor or a peer dumping extra work on you. You should become used to saying "no." There's no need for you to bite off more than you can chew. Instead of being overwhelmed by a large number of duties, prioritize your own.

Final Thoughts

Your productivity and efficiency will contribute to your organization's total production. In addition to keeping yourself productive, you should aim to instil the same mindset in your peers. It is not difficult to become more productive and efficient. You just need to perform what you currently do but in a more effective manner.

Chapter 7.4: Business Management

What can a company do to increase its productivity?

Business productivity is closely tied to a person's level of engagement with their job and employer. According to a new Harvard Business Review research, individuals perform more when someone is observing and appreciating their efforts. Managers and corporate leaders must establish an environment that is inspiring enough to keep employees motivated.

This is particularly critical while working remotely. It is vital to create initiatives that engage people both at work and at home. The more you can pique your team's interest and attention, the higher your chances of increasing production.

10 best ways to improve business productivity

No organization can keep its staff continuously productive unless it has a clear strategy for success. Here are ten of the most successful strategies for increasing effectiveness.

1. Keep things simple

While having a productivity plan is important, it does not have to be complicated. Creating a short, focused strategy with defined actions and results keeps people on track and prepares them for success. Create SMART objectives with concrete, attainable tasks so that everyone is on the same page.

2. Set reminders

Todoist and other smart calendars and reminder applications monitor what has to be done on specified days and times so your brain doesn't have to. More crucially, they may be integrated with collaboration systems like Slack, which allow you to organize by channels, topics, and teams. Set key milestone alerts and notifications at the team level, and allow individuals to create their tasks inside the same channel for more granular things.

3. Goals should be reviewed every day (or at least regularly)

Setting objectives is a critical component of every company plan. They are, however, meaningless unless they are reviewed and amended regularly. After you've established clear objectives, make sure everyone has a mechanism to track progress daily. Set reasonable expectations, such as delivering weekly progress updates or replying within 48 hours, if daily doesn't make sense in a certain case.

4. Minimize time-wasting activities

Numerous distractions might divert our focus away from our tasks, whether at home or work. Successful managers are aware of this and devise strategies to battle the worst of them. Here's how to avoid some of the most prevalent productivity drainers:

- **Meetings**: Limit the number of meetings you have and the people who attend them. If a meeting is required, it should have a clear, focused agenda, and time limitations per subject, and it should finish as soon as a resolution is reached (yes, we want our 15 minutes back!).

- **Emails**: Email is not the only quicker means to obtain or distribute information. Send a short Slack message or direct message, start an impromptu video call, or (gasp) pick up the phone. Direct connection using real-time tools is nearly always more efficient.

- **Coworkers**: While you always want to have a nice relationship with your coworkers, there is a time and place for personal chats. Allow for group lunches, virtual happy hours, topical chat channels, and other activities that encourage individuals to socialize outside of business hours.

- **Lack of organization**: People lose time hunting for what they need due to disorganization (see: 5,000-email inbox). Beyond tidy workstations and labelled files, managing digital processes may significantly boost productivity. Slack, for example, enables you to browse discussions by channel, exchange files inside projects, bookmark critical documents for easier access, and initiate meetings all in one spot.

- **Social media**: People spend approximately two and a half hours every day on social media platforms, according to GlobalWebIndex's "2021 Social Media Trends" research. Establish a policy that specifies when it is OK to use social media and when it is necessary to concentrate on work.

- **Procrastination**: We're all guilty of it. The easiest approach to avoid it is to set clear timelines and hold people accountable. Every individual who has a project deadline should have someone follow up with them to ensure that the deadline is reached. You may also utilize goal-tracking software such as Coach. me or ATracker.

5. Use productivity apps

Technology may be both our greatest asset and our worst distraction. Apps, when utilized correctly, may dramatically increase corporate productivity. Among the most popular productivity applications are:

- Slack
- Todoist
- Dropbox
- Evernote
- Asana

6. Motivate your team

Keeping your team members engaged is one of the most challenging (and vital) company development methods. The "how" will change depending on whomever you ask. As a result, it's critical to grasp what's most essential to each individual you deal with.

Finding a happy medium between inner and external motivation is essential for hitting the productivity sweet spot. Intrinsic motivation creates self-reflective rewards that cause a person to desire to succeed just for their own personal gratification. Extrinsic motivation, on the other hand, gives external incentives for excellent conduct and achievement of objectives, such as more vacation days or a corporate party.

7. Avoid multitasking

Many individuals claim to be superb multitaskers, but in truth, working on one subject at a time is nearly always preferable. Multitasking has been demonstrated in several studies to reduce individual productivity by up to 40%. At the very least, ensure that team members have a generally similar task. Delegate responsibilities based on who is the greatest at them or who is willing to take them on (versus always by role or title). Setting realistic expectations reduces the need to juggle too many things at once or to exert too little effort.

8. Offer a wellness program

Physical and mental health, both of which may boost productivity, are included in wellness. According to the Harvard Business Review, persons with good mental health are 23% more productive, while physically fit employees are 17% more productive.

Weight-loss programs, health tests, and on-site exercise equipment are excellent ways for helping teams increase their overall productivity by concentrating on the full person.

9. Focus on Focus

Employee burnout is a genuine issue in every business. It causes procrastination, a lack of drive, and, in extreme cases, harm and sickness. Vacations may boost physical health, emotional well-being, cognitive performance, and relationships, according to a 2019 research published in the journal Psychology and Health.

Allow for getaways and holidays to keep brains sharp. Provide remote work opportunities to reduce travel weariness. There are several methods for maintaining great contact with your remote workforce while increasing company efficiency.

10. Hold one-on-one meetings

Some individuals find it difficult to freely speak and discuss their thoughts at work, whether with their supervisor or their coworkers. Set up partnerships with members of your team to enhance inclusiveness. Set up frequent in-person meetings or video calls to review workload, objectives, and challenges to improve overall performance and experience.

CHAPTER 8: MASTERPIECE BEING PRODUCTIVE & LIVING PRINCIPLE

Chapter 8.1: How to Find True Happiness and Inner Peace
What Does It Mean to possess Inner Peace and Lasting Happiness?

Knowing inner peace and happiness simply is not the same as possessing them. Ironically, many of us are aware of this concept and may even teach it, yet nothing in our life reflects it.

You may have encountered individuals who constantly look joyful and energetic no matter what occurs, and you wonder whether they could exist in the same world as you. They will almost certainly need to learn the skill of obtaining and maintaining inner serenity. You read it correctly: they must master the art.

Finding inner serenity is not sufficient. The topping is still there. Consider it as a cluttered room - our brains may correctly be compared to a space. You eat, sleep, and add that room, and with everything else going on, you hardly have time to clean it up. You keep putting off packing until you finally decide to do it. It seems to be a brand-new home. The next day, you resume eating and tossing rubbish in the same location, and one week later, you're back at square one.

Steps To Increase Self-Esteem & Find Inner Happiness:

- ❖ **Get to Understand Yourself**

Take some time to get to know yourself and who you are as a person. This practice is often useful for discovering facts about yourself that you may not have known previously!

- ❖ **Remove the Negativity in Your Life**

If something or someone is robbing you of your capacity to feel joyful and tranquil, you must do something to change it or fully eliminate that negativity from your life.

- ❖ **Use Positive Affirmations**

List your favourite positive affirmations in your workbook right away those you believe will be beneficial to you when you're suffering and need some uplifting support.

- ❖ **Get Support**

Make some notes in your notebook and list down whom you're going to solicit support from right now, or how you're going to put yourself out there to make new friends and obtain that support for yourself if it isn't already there.

- ❖ **Give Yourself Grace**

Make an inventory in your workbook, then allow yourself to go forward and overcome these mental obstacles.

- ❖ **Hear What Your Heart Wants**

Listen to your heart nonetheless, and check out to make decisions and choices in your life that are in line with what you genuinely want, not what you think you should desire.

- ❖ **Practice Gratitude**

Gratitude is amusing. As a result, the more you strive to discover it, the more you see and experience it.

Chapter 8.2: How to Work Less and Get More Done

To deal with the modern environment, you must employ the fewest inputs to get the most result. It is proposed to guarantee the efficiency and effectiveness of any job.

In summary, becoming more wiped out in a shorter amount of time so you may leave the workplace early is the greatest way to save time at work. This goal, however, is considerably easier said than done. Fortunately, several tactics may be employed to help anybody, regardless of career, acquire more wiped out in less time.

Step By Step Instructions to Work Less and Accomplish More Work

1. **Apply the 80/20 guideline to your everyday work.**

The 80/20 rule, commonly known as the Pareto Principle, states that 20% of actions account for 80% of the outcomes.

2. **Plan the project and period with Parkinson's Law in mind.**

Parkinson's Law is often stated as "work expands to fill the time available for completion."

3. **Augment productivity by working when you're all around rested and resting when you're drained.**

Working when weary is less effective and often unproductive since we make more errors and create shoddy work when we are sleepy. Instead of pushing yourself to figure, concentrate on working hard (and smartly) while you're well-rested and ensuring that you receive the rest you need to work efficiently.

4. **Don't allow the perfect to be the enemy of the great.**

Attempt to complete tasks when the extra work is offset by a slight increase in the result.

5. **Test your assumptions and tweak your working style as required.**

Throughout your working life, using data, analytics, and A/B testing to continually evaluate your assumptions about what works best will help you uncover and remove inefficiencies in your workflow.

6. **Stick with an even schedule seven days every week.**

To help your body create a consistent habit and begin to be productive at the same time every day. According to Bradberry, sleeping late on weekends disrupts the body's circadian clock, making Mondays that much more unpleasant and less productive.

7. **Seize the morning.**

Changing your wake-up time to a little earlier might boost your overall productivity.

8. **Plan your day the night before.**

A fruitful day does not happen by accident. It necessitates preparation. We are considerably more likely to achieve our objectives if we write down what we want to accomplish and when and where we intend to roll in the hay. So make a plan for your day the night before.

9. **Avoid being 100% booked.**

It's common to believe that the most productive individuals are fully scheduled for the whole day. However, the majority of the folks I've talked with have said the opposite. As a result, you should avoid being completely booked.

Chapter 8.3: Improve Your Work Environment and Optimize Productivity
What is Personal Productivity?

Productivity enhancement has become a societal preoccupation. People desire to work more effectively to be better, quicker, smarter, wealthier, or just to have more time to do activities they like. However, people seldom discuss what it means to be valuable.

Being your most efficient self entails, on a personal level:

> thinking about what you aspire to urge done,
> determining what you're physically capable of destroying in an ideal setting, and
> following through on building an optimum atmosphere and completing the necessary chores to achieve your objectives

Ways to Enhance Your Work Environment and Optimize Productivity

You'll love cleaning up both your desk space and your headspace as a student, employer, employee, and colleague by employing the following hints and tactics.

- ✔ Ritualizing A Piece of Environment
- ✔ Personalizing Your Space
- ✔ Remove Clutter and Therefore the Power of the 'Go-Bag'
- ✔ Keep Your Work Environment Sterile
- ✔ Plants, Open Windows, Air Fresheners
- ✔ Splendour and Lighting – Open Windows and Regular Light
- ✔ Decrease Eye Jerks from Overexposure to Screens
- ✔ Schedule Breaks Without a Clock
- ✔ Neck Pain and Back Strain
- ✔ Water and Snacks
- ✔ Agendas: Observe Little Triumphs and Oversee On-Going Assignments
- ✔ Keep A Well-Balanced Temperature.
- ✔ Use A Calendar
- ✔ Start Every Work Day with An Equivalent Task
- ✔ Tip 16: Write Summaries
- ✔ Keep Applications Silent
- ✔ Socialize

Chapter 8.4: The Secret to Handle Difficult and Toxic People
Do you know someone who is poisonous?

Depleting, unsupportive, and unpleasant people are undoubtedly life's most significant test. Throughout this piece, I'd want to discuss how you can identify, stop, and affect the toxic people in your life. You need people in your life that you love spending time with, who support you, and with whom you want to hang out.

- **The Different kinds of Toxic People**

Have you ever been lectured by someone who constantly interrupts you? Maybe I should rephrase the sentence: have you ever tried to address someone who won't let you finish your sentence? Conversational narcissists like mentioning themselves—or just hearing themselves speak. They don't ask you any questions, they don't wait for your replies, and they won't stop talking. These individuals will be fully self-centred throughout a relationship and will never be aware of your needs.

- **The Strait Jacket**

A straitjacket is someone who wants to control everything and everyone around them. They must accept responsibility for what they do, what they say, and even what they believe. This person will not give you any breathing room and will continue to bother you until you've reached an agreement with them.

- **The Emotional Moocher**

An emotional moocher is also known as a "spiritual vampire" since they tend to drain your optimism or emotionally bleed you dry. These are the folks who are continually saying something sad, negative, or gloomy.

- **The Drama Magnet**

Some poisonous individuals are drama magnets. Usually, something is wrong. Always. When one drag is removed, another appears. and that they are just interested in your understanding, compassion, and support—not your advice! You give assistance and answers, yet they never appear to need anything repaired.

- **The JJ**

A JJ is a person who is envious and judgemental. Envious persons are very toxic because they need so much self-loathing that they can't be happy for anybody around them.

- **The Fibber**

Before I mastered human lie detection, I had a lot of liars in my life. Liars, liars, exaggerators... Having a poisonous deceiver in your life is exhausting.

- **The Tank**

A tank annihilates everything in its path. A person's tank is typically correct, does not regard other people's emotions or opinions, and always prioritizes oneself. while in a relationship They seldom regard people as equals, which will make establishing a romantic bond difficult.

Successful Ways People Handle Toxic People

- Limit Your Time and Energy with Chronic Complainers
- Pick Your Battles with Toxic People Wisely
- Don't Get Sucked into Irrational Behavior
- Don't Let People Push Their Buttons
- Try to establish Your Boundaries
- Don't try to Let Others Limit Their Joy.
- Try to Specialize in Solution Rather Than Fixing Problems
- Understand how to forgive but not forget
- Don't Engage in Negative Self-Talk
- Hamper on Caffeine.
- Try to Have Enough Sleep
- belief in Friends and Family
- Learn to Adapt

Chapter 8.5: How to Build and Sustain a Healthy and Purposeful Relationship

Why is it important to create healthy positive relationships?

Understanding the best way to enhance good connections and prevent negative connections is critical to living a vibrant and full life. There are several advantages to having a good happy relationship:

- ✔ *It encourages personal growth*
- ✔ *It provides support for you in adversity*
- ✔ *It helps reduce stress*
- ✔ *It provides an opportunity to collaborate*
- ✔ *It helps you develop healthy behaviour*
- ✔ *It adds more aim to life*

What are the consequences of toxic relationships?

A toxic relationship depletes your life, harms your self-esteem, or destroys your aspirations. While this may seem to be fatal, toxic relationships are frequently subtle and do significant damage before you realize it.

- ✔ *It destroys your self-esteem and self-confidence.*
- ✔ *It consumes your energy.*
- ✔ *It breeds negativity.*
- ✔ *It increases your stress level*

✔ *It affects your other relationships.*
Tips To Create and Sustain Meaningful Relationships

Let's get right into the concepts that could help you develop and maintain a meaningful, healthy, and good relationship.

1. Fall Crazy with Yourself.
    - Learn To Concentrate and Understand.
    - Always Follow-Up.
    - Find Common Interests.
    - Communicate What You Would Like.
    - Always Be Wanting to Help
    - Learn to Trust Others
    - Identify and Avoid Interpersonal Pitfalls.
    - Don't Be the Judge
    - Let It Out and Let It Go
    - Do Regular Checks of The Relationships You've Got.
    - Twiddling My Thumbs.

www.ingramcontent.com/pod-product-compliance
Lightning Source LLC
Chambersburg PA
CBHW072102110526
44590CB00018B/3287